Trading with Ichimoku Clouds

Founded in 1807, John Wiley & Sons is the oldest independent publishing company in the United States. With offices in North America, Europe, Australia and Asia, Wiley is globally committed to developing and marketing print and electronic products and services for our customers' professional and personal knowledge and understanding.

The Wiley Trading series features books by traders who have survived the market's ever changing temperament and have prospered—some by reinventing systems, others by getting back to basics. Whether a novice trader, professional or somewhere in-between, these books will provide the advice and strategies needed to prosper today and well into the future.

For a list of available titles, visit our Web site at www.WileyFinance.com.

Trading with Ichimoku Clouds

The Essential Guide to Ichimoku Kinko Hyo Technical Analysis

MANESH PATEL

WILEY

John Wiley & Sons, Inc.

Published by John Wiley & Sons, Inc., Hoboken, New Jersey.
Published simultaneously in Canada.

Charts used with permission of TradeStation, Inc.

For general information on our other products and services or for technical support, please contact our Customer Care Department within the United States at (800) 762-2974, outside the United States at (317) 572-3993 or fax (317) 572-4002.

Wiley also publishes its books in a variety of electronic formats. Some content that appears in print may not be available in electronic books. For more information about Wiley products, visit our web site at www.wiley.com.

Library of Congress Cataloging-in-Publication Data:

Patel, Manesh.
    Trading with Ichimoku clouds : the essential guide to Ichimoku Kinko Hyo technical analysis / Manesh Patel.
        p. cm. – (Wiley trading series)
    Includes bibliographical references and index.
    ISBN 978-0-470-60993-4 (cloth)
    1. Investment analysis.   2. Stocks–Prices–Charts, diagrams, etc.   I. Title.
    HG4529.P38 2010
    332.63'2042–dc22
                                                                    2009052168

10 9 8 7 6 5 4 3 2 1

I am dedicating this book to my late father
Ramanlal K. Patel—a father who encouraged me to
be the best I can and to follow my dreams.
If it were not for him, I would not be who I am today.

A portion of the proceeds from this book will be given to various charities around the world in his name.

Contents

Introduction

BACKGROUND

"Japanese Candles" is a phrase that is well known among the trading community. If the phrase is searched on the Internet, 3,810,000 searches are available in the Google search engine today. In comparison, if "Ichimoku" is searched, 141,000 searches appear, which is quite a difference. Steve Nison brought Japanese Candlesticks to the Western world and did a great job illustrating how it can be used to become a successful trader. He left a huge mark on the trading community, and today institutions down to the average retail trader use Japanese Candlesticks in some form or fashion in their technical analysis.

This book brings the next phrase of Japanese technical analysis to the Western world, "Ichimoku Kinko Hyo." Ichimoku Kinko Hyo is a system that has been used successfully throughout Japan for years but never has progressed forward in the Western world. If a trader combines Japanese Candles with Ichimoku Kinko Hyo, a powerful system is available to him or her. In fact, it increases the probability of trading drastically and can be evidenced by trading in a "paper" account after reading this book. Japanese Candlesticks will not be discussed further in this book and any additional information regarding this topic is available through Steve Nison's books and training seminars.

By the time this book is published, the market will be one that has not been experienced previously; not even historical traders can predict what the future holds. There are no historical references to the current market models. We have seen the volatility index (VIX) (Figure I.1), which averaged a value of 10 to 12 for a number of years in the middle of this decade, and exceeded 50 for the first time during the collapse of the global financial markets. Why is this market different from any other historical period?

One of the biggest reasons that the market is so different is technology. With the advent of the Internet, information can be received *globally* in a matter of milliseconds. During the crash of 1929, no computers were available and television was in its early stages. The first televised live broadcast from a plane had just occurred. Two years earlier, the biggest news

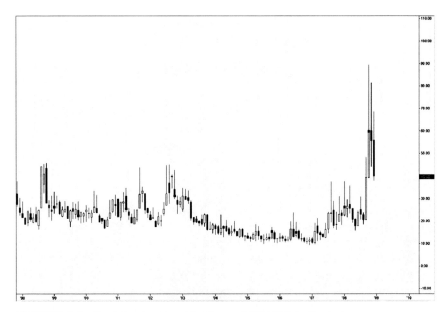

FIGURE I.1   TradeStation Monthly Chart of $VIX.X Volatility Index

worldwide was: "In 1927, the president of the American Telephone and Telegraph Company in New York talked by phone to Herbert Hoover in Washington, more than 200 miles away. The president of the telephone company was able to see clearly the face of Mr. Hoover as he talked. This proved to the world that electricity could be used to carry sight as well as sound."

During the mid-1980s, computers were still in their early stages. It was the beginning of the personal computer era—Microsoft was introducing the operation system MS-DOS 3.2, Apple was introducing the Mac Plus, IBM was launching the first laptop computer, and so forth. Technology began to advance drastically in a short period. The size of a microchip was getting smaller and smaller and the computing power within the microchip was exponentially increasing in a short amount of time. What normally took a room full of technological resources to do was now available in the size of a desktop computer.

A perfect example of the rapid change in technology is mainframes. Back in the 1970s, IBM dominated the mainframe "space." Mainframes were performing the computing power needed by various industry groups. It would normally take an entire room size of more than 1,000 square feet just to be able to store this technology. Not only that, the room needed the ability to store all the cabling and also required the support of a high-powered cooling system. The expense associated with mainframes was in the magnitude of more than $100,000. Only big corporations and universities could afford such "luxuries." Small companies had to perform calculations by hand or they had to hire some of these larger corporations to perform the task they needed. With the introduction of personal computers in the mid-1980s, small companies and private individuals were now able to directly participate in the computer era. Prices dropped from a six-figure number to a magnitude of $3,000 to $5,000. My personal experience back in the 1980s was with the Apple IIE and then progressed forward with the IBM XT machines with Microsoft DOS. These were the days where there really was no graphical interface and everything was in the form of pure text.

In the 1990s, technology introduced the concept of the Internet and the World Wide Web. A drastic event in a small town in India now can be heard and seen throughout the world in a matter of seconds. Information traveled the world in microseconds compared to days/weeks/months as it did in earlier decades. In regard to the financial markets, one event in a particular market caused an instant "chain reaction" across all financial markets globally within a short amount of time. Not only can the events occur instantly but they can also affect everyone, that is, lower, middle, and upper classes worldwide. By the late 1990s, almost every individual around the world had some sort of investment in some financial market, either through an online real-time brokerage account, money market account, CD, retirement account (401(k)), and so forth. Control was now in the hands of an emotional retail customer compared to a professional trader.

In this book, you learn the key aspects of becoming a professional trader. I walk you through the complete process of trading with Ichimoku Kinko Hyo. After you read the book, various resources are available to you to make sure that your journey into the "Ichimoku world" is successful.

Types of Trading

In order to trade, two key questions always need to be addressed:

Question 1: When and what price should we enter the trade?
Question 2: When and what price should we exit a trade?

There are two analytical models—Technical Analysis and Fundamental Analysis—that help the trader get the answers to these questions. Technical analysis consists of looking at price and time action for a particular instrument. Today, online brokerage accounts along with other firms offer a retail customer hundreds of indicators for price and time analysis. The indicators are sometimes called "studies" and they are mathematical formulas that represent price and time action in a certain way. With a certain rule set, the graphical indicator tells a trader key information on what has been happening with price over a certain time period. Examples of some indicators are Moving Averages, Average True Range (ATR), Stochastic, Pivot points, and so forth.

Hundreds of different strategies can be found with these indicators. Strategies take the various indicators and come up with a certain set of rules that the trader can follow to trade. Infinite numbers of possible strategies can be created for a trading system by a trader with the hundreds of indicators available. Furthermore, some strategies focus only on certain markets and on certain time frames. The days of trading based on a simple strategy are gone! Technical charts are now cluttered with indicators, lines, text, graphical objects, and so forth. The charts are so cluttered that it is hard for anyone new to understand a chart at "first glance." It takes days and even months for someone to understand how to trade based on someone's trading system.

My background is engineering and as a result, I tend to overcomplicate things as many engineers have a tendency to do. Before the days of Ichimoku Kinko Hyo, I mainly traded stocks. If someone looked at my charts before I adopted Ichimoku Kinko Hyo, he or she would be completely confused. In performing a technical analysis, I would first start by drawing Fibonacci lines and Gann lines. If this revealed a possible entry, I would then look at the Commodity Channel Indicator (CCI), the Average True Range indicator, and the stochastic indicator. If I got a "green light" from *those* indicators then I would look at the *market indexes* and see if it supported my decision in the direction I planned to take.

I never wanted to trade against the market in general and as a result, I would look at the Trading Index Indicator (TRIN) and then analyze the S&P futures with Fibonacci/Gann/CCI/ATR, and so forth. If everything "lined up" on my two-monitor screen, then I moved forward to trade based on pivots. I hope that everyone followed that because I was insane back in those days. I look back and wonder how I understood the complicated process that I created. That is a lot of work just to analyze *one* stock. You can image how hard it was to analyze all 5,000-plus stock instruments. One person stated it perfectly to me when they saw my screens: "death by indicators."

Unlike technical analysis, which is graphical, the second analytical model—fundamental analysis—is based on numbers. Let us first look at fundamental analysis for stocks and how it is used. In fundamental valuation for stocks, you are looking to buy a stock based on that company's being undervalued. In order to determine if a company is being undervalued, a "fair value" for a company needs to be determined. Some traders may use a Profit/Earnings (P/E) ratio to determine whether to purchase a stock. For example, if a P/E ratio of 10 is used, then any stock at a P/E of 10 or less could be purchased.

One of the key things I look at is the 10 P/E ratio level on a chart. If you see a P/E ratio of 10, normally you see technical support in that particular stock. Other variations that may be used are stocks at a P/E level of 10 or less as well as Cash to Short Term (ST) Liability's level of 50 percent. This would indicate the stock is trading at a low earnings multiple. The stock is well funded in terms of its debt exposure. All of this obviously has nothing to do with technicals or charting—it's financial company analysis. But when overlying these stocks onto a chart you may be able to apply support levels to this fundamental analysis.

Today, if you listen to the news, you will see that many companies provide many revisions to their numbers and also many companies are "cooking the books." They manipulate numbers before earnings announcements just to drive the stock price higher. Based on these manipulated values, fundamentalists will buy/sell the stock. If the truth comes out, their investment will be destroyed completely. In the last couple of years, many companies have been getting in trouble based on "accounting practices." How can you trust the results if this is happening more and more often? Let us say that a company is not manipulating the numbers and they announce a good quarter, why does a stock go down when they beat estimates and have good fundamental values? Why will some instruments move more than 20 percent faster than their earnings percentage growth? There is no direct answer to these questions. Everything depends on speculation, which is not predictable. Here is an article in *USA Today* on June 27, 2002, on a company called WorldCom:

> *WorldCom's accounting game is stunning investors who thought the loophole the telecom firm used was sewn shut years ago.*
>
> *Showing that accounting gimmicks may fade but never really go away, WorldCom acknowledged it improperly "capitalized" costs. This shenanigan was believed to be one that is quickly detected by analysts and, if not, used to fudge books by much smaller amounts.*
>
> *"This had been a huge problem at one time, but it has receded over the years," says Robert Willens of Lehman Bros. "How was this overlooked by people who are supposed to be looking at it?" he asks.*
>
> *WorldCom used the gimmick to a level never before seen. The company showed a $1.4 billion profit in 2001, rather than a loss, by using what's essentially the oldest trick in the book.*
>
> *Rather than subtracting certain costs—which analysts think were for maintaining telecom systems—from profit, it called them long-term investments. Doing this allowed WorldCom to inflate*

earnings because the costs of long-term investments are subtracted
from earnings over time, rather than all at once up front.
   WorldCom wouldn't say which costs were incorrectly recorded
   Things to keep in mind about improper capitalization:
   High-profile companies have pulled it off before. It's an easy way
for high-growth companies to delay recording costs, says Howard
Schilit, president of the Center for Financial Research & Analysis.
   For instance, America Online paid a $3.5 million fine to the Se-
curities and Exchange Commission in 2000 to settle charges it cap-
italized the costs of mailing out thousands of trial diskettes in the
mid-'90s.
   The SEC found that by not charging the expense right away, AOL
reported a profit instead of a loss for three years. AOL says it stopped
capitalizing the costs in October 1996 because it changed its busi-
ness model. "This was completely different, as AOL's accounting was
always fully disclosed and AOL did not admit any wrongdoing in its
settlement agreement," says spokeswoman Ann Brackbill.
   Any company in any industry can use the tactic.

We have discussed fundamental analysis for stocks but are the currencies the same? How do you now apply fundamental analysis to trading
currencies? In order to answer this question, central bank policies need to
be discussed. First, there is hawkish (which is a bias toward raising interest rates). A bank can do this to stop inflation, to reduce money supply,
and so forth. Normally if the future of a currency has higher interest rates,
then the value of that currency should increase. Next, there is a central
bank policy that is dovish (which is bias toward lowering interest rates).
This policy is used to increase money supply, help stimulate an economy,
and so forth. If you can find a currency pair with one country being dovish
and another being hawkish then you have a great currency trade from a
fundamental viewpoint. For example, in the past few years, the Japanese
yen (Japan had a Zero Interest Rate Policy) versus almost any currency.
If you have ever heard of the famous concept "carry trade," it is dealing
with the Japanese yen and other currency pairs. Since the financial market
meltdown, the United States has had a policy of keeping rates under 1 percent for an extended period of time. As a result, the U.S. dollar is a carry
trade with the Japanese yen and has subsequently led to a decline in the
U.S. dollar.
   So far, fundamental analysis for stocks and currencies has been discussed and it is apparent that you have to know a lot of information in
order to trade stocks and currencies with this approach. How do the other
instruments such as commodity futures (Corn, Wheat, Soybeans, Feeder
Cattle, and so forth) fare with fundamental analysis? If you are trading all

these instruments, you have to have a "global" view of everything that is going on in the world in order to trade. Some traders have taken the time to learn, especially with the Internet; however, for many people that is virtually impossible.

The main goal of this book is to *simplify* trading. All the fundamental aspects of each instrument and market will be built into price. Therefore, we are only going to rely on price action on the charts to determine when to trade and when not to trade. This is the assumption behind Ichimoku Kinko Hyo, a technical system. If you are a fundamental trader, my suggestion would be to combine the technical and fundamental analysis together as part of your trading system. Remember, *your* trading system has to be something you are comfortable with and fits your "personality." Anything short of that will be *failure*.

Now, we are going to proceed forward and start to create the foundation "blocks" for you to become a professional trader using the Ichimoku Kinko Hyo system.

COMPONENTS OF A TRADING SYSTEM

Trading and investing are very simple processes and we human beings try to make it into something much more complex. Unfortunately, we have a lot of biases that enter into trading decisions.

I believe people get exactly what they want out of the markets and most people are afraid of success or failure. As a result, they tend to resist change and continue to follow their natural biases and lose in the markets. When you get rid of the fear, you tend to get rid of the biases.

As for risk, most people don't understand it, including a lot of professionals, and what's really interesting is that once you understand risk and portfolio management, you can design a trading system with almost any level of performance.

—Van K. Tharp

Background

People can learn a lot about life by observing nature's creatures, observations that can benefit every aspect of someone's life. Let us examine a cougar and how it hunts for prey. The cougar is one of nature's fiercest creatures. When hunting for prey, a cougar is strategic. If a cougar finds a herd of deer, it will wait patiently observing the entire herd looking for the weakness within the herd. The reason for this is that the cougar can only run at top speed for short distances. Therefore, it is imperative to get as close to its prey as possible before making a killing strike. Otherwise, the opportunity will be lost and it may be some time before the next one appears. The more days that the cougar goes without food, the slower it will be able to run, thus making it harder and harder to attack its prey.

So why are we talking about cougars?

Playing the market is very much like the cougar's hunt for prey. Whether you are trading the Forex market, the Futures market, the Options market, the Equities market, and so forth, you must have a *plan* before entering each trade. If you do not, it will be harder and harder to find opportunities because each lost opportunity will take a toll mentally, physically, and psychologically on your well-being.

Therefore, you must observe the instrument greatly before executing a trade. In another words, you must become an *analyst* before a trader. If you are a trader before an analyst then you will be "rolling dice" at each opportunity. Just like the cougar observes its prey for weaknesses before becoming a hunter, you must analyze before trading, otherwise success will get further and further away.

An analyst observes the instrument *patiently* until an opportunity is seen. Once an opportunity is present, a plan is executed. The plan consists of entry criteria, money management, and so forth. Figure I.2 is an example of a good trading plan. A true trader will not play a "probability game" but instead wait for the market to "show" him or her the opportunity through patience and discipline.

Someone once told me "Trading is neither logical nor predictable." After years of trading, I can honestly say that statement is completely true. It

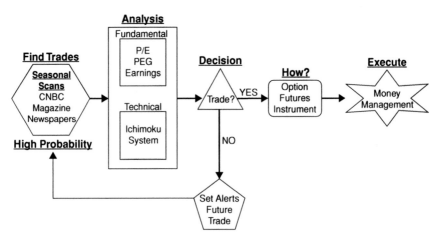

FIGURE I.2 Trading Plan Example

is a probability game. You have to have a system to help increase your probability of success or you are just gambling. By rolling a dice, a person has a probability of 50 percent on the desired outcome. Therefore, one of our goals is to trade with a higher probability of success than 50 percent. How do you do that? This can be achieved by creating a trading system that maximizes profits when you are right and minimizes losses when you are wrong (i.e., play trends instead of consolidation patterns). A trend is when price goes in a certain direction for a long period of time whereas a consolidation pattern is where price goes "back and forth" among a range of prices.

Trading Plan   My mentor always stated the following: "A System without a proper mind set leads to ruin; however, the proper mind set perfectly aligned with the right mind set leads to Success."

When evaluating trading systems and plans, we always ask the following two questions:

1. Does the system/plan cover the mind set required to trade the system?
2. Does the system/plan cover the personality required to trade the system?

Why do we ask these questions? There are many different trading plans out there. Each plan requires a particular mind set and personality from the trader using the system. Does your plan match your personality and mindset? If not then you are bound to fail. *Take the time to find what works for you!* If the trading plan we create in this book is not for you then change it so you are comfortable with it. Do not use it if you are not comfortable with it.

The first component of the trading system is the trading plan. A trading plan is where you take a certain strategy and execute it with a certain set of rules. It takes all the emotions and decision-making process completely out so someone just has to follow the trading plan and play the odds. The majority of retail traders today do not have a trading plan and are "blindly" trading. Without a plan, they are gambling instead of system trading. All they know is that they want to make money. Therefore, they go through a trial and error scenario to find a strategy that works for them. If by chance, the strategy starts to fail, they drop that strategy and seek another one. They switch strategies as much as the "mood" changes in the market. This is a dangerous strategy because if volatility is high then the market is swinging up and down drastically. As a result, there will be no consistency in trading. Without consistency, traders become less patient and the less patient a person is, the higher the probability that a mistake will be made (i.e., higher losses). This is a vicious cycle that many cannot escape!

FIGURE I.3 TradeStation Daily Chart, Daily Chart of $INDU February 27, 2007

A perfect example of this is shown in Figure I.3. It is a chart of the Dow Jones Industrial Average on May 1, 2007. On this date, the market went down drastically and there was a massive sell-off as people panicked. A few months later on April 18, 2007, the market had completely retraced 100 percent back to the original price before the big drop. In fact, the market continued to proceed higher. How many people do you think had a trading plan on February 27, 2007? How many people had "built-in" stops?

If you examine the price action before this major drop, you will see that the markets have been going higher and higher for the last couple of years. Before February 2007, the market had been in a major bull run. The price action set a mode of "quick easy cash" mentality. People could buy and walk away and expect a 10 percent average yearly profit, which was three times more than a money market savings account. Many people thought it was a "sure bet" that they started to use margin to hold positions for that quick percentage return. They did this in their regular brokerage accounts along with their retirement accounts. When the market decided to correct itself, a couple of down days caused major panic across the globe. It happened in the stock market, currency market, bond market, commodity market, and so forth. The big daily down bar is the panic that took place. The people who had a trading plan most likely were out before that major down day occurred. If you were trading with Ichimoku, you would have

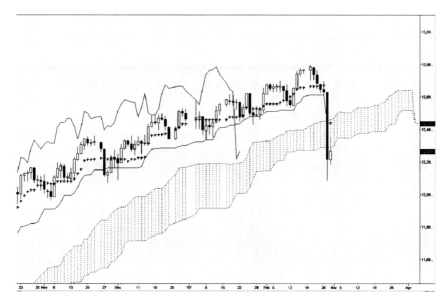

FIGURE I.4 TradeStation Daily Ichimoku Chart, Chart of $INDU Feb 28, 2007

been out of the market either one or two days before the major down day (Figure I.4).

A trading plan should consist of the following four components:

1. What instruments will be traded and when?
    a. Instrument examples: Stock, Exchange-Traded Funds, Option, Future, and so forth.
    b. Time frame: Tick, 1 minute, 3 minutes, 120 minutes, daily, weekly
2. Entry Rules:
    a. Fundamental: PEG, PE, Cash flow, and so forth
    b. Technical Analysis: Ichimoku, Moving Average, Average True Range, Fibonacci, Gann Theory, Pivots, Volume Spread analysis, and so forth
3. Money Management:
    a. Stop: If you are wrong, where will you get out of the trade? Believe it or not, there are many traders who do not use a stop at all. They are fearful that the brokers/market makers will see their stop and run the price to hit all the stops. That is true in some cases especially if you are trading lower time frames. However, what will happen to your account if a news announcement comes and moves price drastically in a matter of milliseconds? With the use of an automated

trading system with the latest technology, millions of trades can now be executed in less than one second! Do you want to be on the other side of the trade?

Notice, I have used the word "stop" compared to "stop loss." In my mentoring, the biggest obstacle for someone to overcome is the psychology of the word "loss" in "stop loss." The word "loss" has a negative meaning that people fear and try to avoid. When it does occur, the person's state of mind is altered to a point where logical thinking no longer occurs and "panic" sets in. Many people believe they do not panic when they have a loss but there are many forms of panic.

Here is a great analogy to prove the point:

In elementary school, there are two boys, the first boy's name is Ben and the second boy's name is Frank. Frank has a perfect attendance and is proud of his accomplishment and strives every day to make sure he maintains that status. One day, Frank was walking to school as he *normally* does each day. As he was walking, another boy named Ben approaches Frank. Ben hits Frank in the stomach for no apparent reason and then walks away. Frank does not understand why Ben did that so he does not take any action. The second day Frank walks to school and runs into Ben again. Again, Ben hits Frank in the stomach and then walks away. The third day comes and Frank, who is afraid of getting hit, decides to take another route to school in order to avoid Ben. Frank avoids Ben but he arrives to school late. The route he had to take was a route that took longer than he expected. His perfect attendance was ruined in one day due to Ben!

So what is the moral? Frank got hit once but kept on following his plan to go to school as he normally does. When the second time occurred, he was cautious but not prepared because he did not think it would happen again but it did. The third time, he reacted but he lost his perfect attendance. He was so worried about Ben he forgot about this perfect attendance, which was important to him.

When trading, if you view the word "stop" as a loss, it is a negative state of mind. If it occurs once, twice, three times, and so on, sooner or later it will alter your state of mind to a point where you will start to react to it instead of following your "game plan." If you get stopped out of a trade that means *you were wrong*. Remember, the goal is to have a trading strategy that minimizes losses when you are wrong and maximizes profits when you are right. Notice I said minimize not *none*? Using the word "none" is not real, it is a dream world.

b. Profit target: Some strategies use a profit target and some don't. It is a not a *must* compared to a Stop.

c. Position sizing: As the trend develops, you have an option of adding or removing positions. One strategy is where you enter the initial position with a low contract/share size. This is done to lower risk and to "test the field." If the trend develops then you add more and more positions on pullbacks. The second strategy is the reverse of the first one and you start with a large number of contracts/shares. As the trend develops, you remove positions at major support/resistance values. Each position sizing strategy has its pro/cons. You can research both types further; however, remember, you *must* select a plan that fits your personality. If you do not like risk at all then *do not* do any position sizing or any scaling in (adding) as the trend develops.

d. Time Entry/Exit: Some strategies focus around time. They typically do this because volume is high or low during the trading time of interest.

e. Money Management

i. Risk per Trade: These parameters define the most risk that a trader is willing to take per trade. If the trade is long term, the risk per trade will be higher compared to someone who is trading on a short-term time frame. For example, most people who trade daily charts for currencies have a max risk of 200 pips per trade. They are willing to accept this value because they are expecting to be in a trade for one month to four months averaging around 400-plus pip profit. They are expecting a 2:1 profit/risk ratio on the trade. So why does this matter? The reason is that we are trading a *system* and not gambling. Everything is defined in a system so you are playing the "numbers." If you have a loss on two trades and win on another trade, you know that at least you will break even because the one win provided 400 pips in profit and the two losses totaled 400 pips. Together, it equals zero. Therefore, your worst-case scenario is one winning trade takes care of two losses.

ii. Risk per Month: The risk per month should be based on the percentage of capital you have to invest. You want to make sure that you do not lose all your money in one month and end up without any cash to trade another month. Remember, you have to treat this like a business. There *will be* some negative months due to the market consolidating. During those times, your system is supposed to minimize the losses. During trend months, your system is supposed to maximize profits. Risk per month can also be called "drawn down."

   iii. Risk/Reward Ratio: The risk/reward ratio is an important calcu-
        lation. It is key because we are trading a trend system. The goal
        of a trend system is to maximize profits when you are right and
        minimize losses when you are wrong. In order to achieve this,
        the risk/reward ratio for your system has to be less than one. No-
        tice, I said *your system*. You may have some trades that have a
        Risk/Reward ratio greater than one, but overall, the backtest re-
        sults should show your system has a risk/reward ratio less than
        one. In theory, if you can optimize your system to a point where
        all trades have a risk/reward of less than one, then you have a
        great system. This can only happen with time as you learn more
        about the optimization part of backtesting.

4. Trade Post Analysis: Probability Factor, Risk/Reward Analysis, Loss
   Analysis. In a later chapter, we illustrate how to "backtest" a system.
   Once the system has been backtested, you can get a lot of information
   from the backtest results. The results should show you the probability
   of winning compared to losing, average Risk/Reward per trade, and so
   forth. Information that should be used to determine whether the system needs to be "tweaked" or optimized. For example, if you are looking for a 12 percent return a year then your backtest results should
   give an average of 12.0 percent per year. If it does not then the system
   needs to be altered in order to achieve your long-term goals. Once the
   system backtest results meet the entire trader's requirements, the system is traded in a live environment with actual cash. Now, the results
   need to be recorded for the live account because what has happened
   in the past does not necessarily mean it will occur in the future. Therefore, post analysis of the trades has to be maintained to verify that the
   system will produce the long-term goals of your business.

Remember, a trading plan is like a business plan to a business, it is a
must and the key for a business to be successful.

In this book, we learn the Ichimoku Kinko Hyo trading system. A trading plan is created step by step around one Ichimoku Kinko Hyo strategy.

Technical Systems   The second component for our trading system
is going to be the technical analysis component. So what is a technical
system? Is it Fibonacci? Is it Gann boxes? Is it Pivot Points? Fibonacci,
Gann boxes, Pivot Points, and so forth, are some forms of support and
resistance values. In fact, every technical system is some form of support
and resistance.

So what is support and resistance? Support is when a user is short a
position in the market (betting on the instrument going down) and price

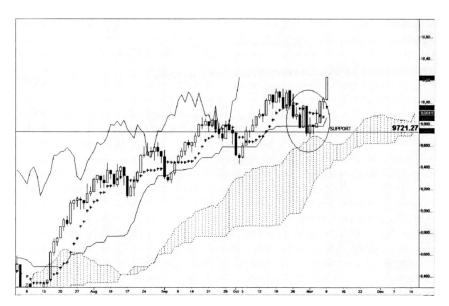

FIGURE I.5 TradeStation Daily Ichimoku Chart, Chart of $INDU Nov 9, 2009

gets to a value (i.e., support price where it cannot go lower at all). If it is a strong support level then price will reverse off that value and start to go *higher* (Figure I.5). Support is referred to by traders as the "floor."

Resistance is when a user is long a position in the market (betting on the instrument going up) and price gets to a value, that is, resistance price where it cannot seem to higher at all (Figure I.6). If it is a strong resistance level then price will reverse off that value and start to go *lower*. Resistance is referred to by traders as the "ceiling."

If everything is based on support and resistance then why not use a technical system that is simple, one that shows all the minor and major support and resistance values? Ichimoku Kinko Hyo is a technical system that illustrates support and resistance values in a simplified form. In fact, the system was built on the idea that at "one glance" you should be able to determine whether an instrument is in equilibrium (consolidation) or out of equilibrium (trending).

The most valuable aspect of Ichimoku Kinko Hyo is that it looks for history to repeat itself now and also in the future. Through the Ichimoku charts, you can see past "events" easily and make current decisions based on past events. W.D. Gann, one of the most successful traders of all time, studied past events in order to determine future events. Ichimoku allows the trader to do the same. It shows the past, present, and the future (Figure I.7) through its five indicators. Some people will argue that past events

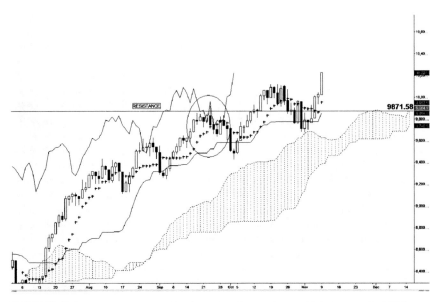

FIGURE I.6   TradeStation Daily Ichimoku Chart, Chart of $INDU Nov 9, 2009

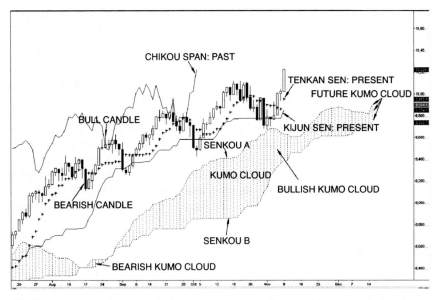

FIGURE I.7   TradeStation Daily Ichimoku Chart, Chart of $INDU Nov 9, 2009

will not necessarily repeat in the future. That is true but how else can we increase the probability of success? This is the best way to increase the probability of success in trading.

In this book, we are not going to discuss the history of Ichimoku Kinko Hyo in great detail. *Ichimoku Charts: An Introduction to Ichimoku Kinko Clouds* from Nicole Elliott is the best place to discover the origin of the Ichimoku Kinko Hyo System. It goes through details on how Goichi Hosada discovered Ichimoku Kinko Hyo in 1948 to Hidenobu Sasaki, the person who wrote a book about Ichimoku Kinko Hyo in Japanese. It is not important for us to learn how he created the system to use it. It is important for us to learn the system and know how to use it to become a successful trader. Therefore, we will not focus on this topic at all.

The next section talks about all the individual components that make up the Ichimoku Kinko Hyo system. Everyone must understand the individual components of Ichimoku in order to be a successful trader. Many traders choose to use only one or two of the Ichimoku components to trade. That is fine but everyone should learn all the components at some point in order to understand what indicator is used to determine what piece of information. You have to realize why there are five components to Ichimoku compared to two or three.

## CHAPTER 1

Ichimoku
Components

Before I start to explain all the Ichimoku components, I need to discuss some background information. First, I use the *daily* time frame as the main reference time frame throughout the book. However, this does not mean that Ichimoku Kinko Hyo only works for the daily time frame. Today, Ichimoku is used at the tick level, 1 minute, 3 minutes, 5 minutes, 60 minutes, 120 minutes, daily, weekly, and so forth. The reason why I discuss the daily time frame is that everything moves at a "slower pace" than the minute time frame. You can "see" everything this way. In order to be able to trade a faster time frame like a 5 minute, you *must* master the daily time frame.

The next question everyone asks now is: Should we look at a lower time frame along with the daily time frame? To answer that question you have to look at the three different types of trades that exist:

1. Trend: Price goes in one direction for a long period of time. During a trend, the higher time frames *influence* the lower time frames where the lower time frames are supporting the higher time frames (Figure 1.1).

2. Countertrend: Price has gone in a certain direction for a long time *already*. Now, the trader believes that the trend is over and the trader wants to trade *against* the trend. During a countertrend movement, the lower time frames *are not* supporting the trend. They are going against the trend to a point they *influence* the high time frames (Figure 1.2).

1

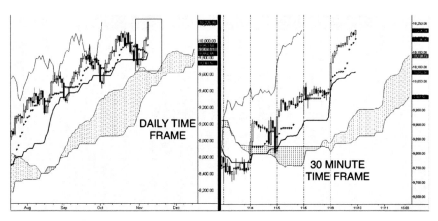

FIGURE 1.1 TradeStation Daily Ichimoku Chart/30 m Chart of $INDU Nov 9, 2009

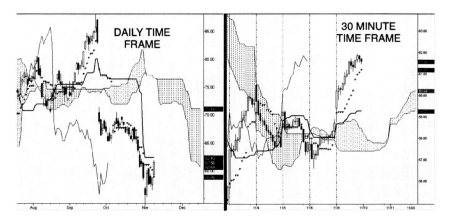

FIGURE 1.2 TradeStation Daily Ichimoku Chart/30 m Chart of RIMM Nov 9, 2009

   3. Consolidation: Price is not going in one particular direction at all. It
      is going back and forth between major support and resistance values
      (Figure 1.3).

   If you do not know how to recognize whether an instrument is trending, in a countertrend mode, or a consolidation mode then you will get confused when you look at the lower time frames. Using multiple time frames
is an advance optimization technique. Once you trade the daily time frame
for a while, you will learn when price is trending, going against the trend,
or in a consolidation pattern.

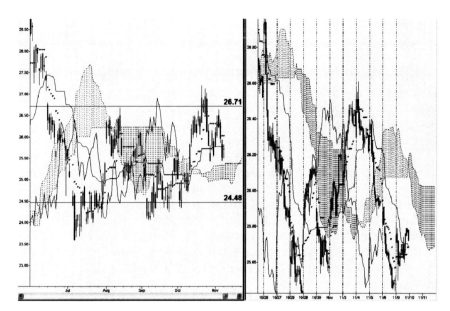

FIGURE 1.3 TradeStation Daily Ichimoku Chart/30m Chart of DBA Nov 9, 2009

The Ichimoku Kinko Hyo system is made up of five components (Figure 1.4):

1. Tenkan Sen (red)
2. Kijun Sen (green)
3. Chikou Span (light purple)

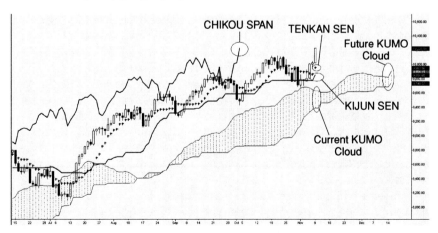

FIGURE 1.4 TradeStation Daily Ichimoku Chart of $INDU Nov 13, 2009

4. Senkou A

5. Senkou B

In the book, all the pictures will be in black and white. However, all charts on my web site (www.eiicapital.com) are color-coded. I have included the color codes for the various indicators that I use on a normal day-to-day basis so you will be able to recognize them on the web site.

The Ichimoku five components together tell the entire "story" behind the chart for a particular instrument. Many people have tried to use only two or three components and have failed miserably. The key for an Ichimoku trader is to understand each element individually and then understand how and why they work together. Once you master that, you will be able to trade Ichimoku with no problems.

In addition, the indicators are referenced based on price, not time. There is a time element to Ichimoku Kinko Hyo, which is discussed in a later section.

TENKAN SEN

The first indicator I discuss is the Tenkan Sen. It represents the short-term movement for price. The color that represents the Tenkan Sen is red. The formula for the Tenkan Sen (red) is:

$$\frac{(\text{Highest High} + \text{Lowest Low})}{2} \text{ for 9 periods}$$

Most retail and institution traders use a 10 period simple moving average of closing prices (SMA) to represent the short term. By using the average of the Highest High and the Lowest Low instead of the closing prices, the Tenkan Sen takes into account the inter-day volatility.

Figure 1.5 shows both the Tenkan Sen and a 9 period SMA for the Europe-USD dollar (EURUSD). Notice during the trend the Tenkan Sen did not go above the inter-day low except for one time, whereas the 9 period SMA penetrated the inter-day low more than nine times. By using the average of the Highest High and the Lowest Low instead of closing prices, the Tenkan reflects short-term price movement better. In fact, you can use the Tenkan as a *stop* once you have entered a trade. For beginners, a stop is where you will get out of a trade if you made a mistake (i.e., the risk of the trade). When you place an order, you should always have a stop order against the entry order so if you are wrong, the trade will automatically

FIGURE 1.5   TradeStation Daily Ichimoku Chart of EURUSD Nov 9, 2009

exit. Many people lose all their money in their accounts because they forget or did not want to place a Stop order. *You have to place a stop order to be a successful trader.*

One question I get all the time is: Why a 9 period? Why not 10, which reflects the trading days in the week or two weeks? That is a good question and really there is no right answer for it. When Ichimoku was first invented in Japan, nine was chosen to reflect the trading days for that period of time. Times have changed so people think that this value should be changed, too. I have not experimented with other period values for any of the Ichimoku indicators as others have done so already. *I do not* plan to do so in the future either. I would rather spend my time analyzing charts and working with the parameters that have worked and been proven over time. There are five Ichimoku indicators. If you change one formula then you will have to adjust the other formulas. How many different combinations do you think there are when you have to alter all five indicators periods? There are thousands . . .

For the Tenkan Sen, there are a few things to note:

- Sentiment
  - *Bullish*: If price is above the Tenkan Sen (Figure 1.6).
  - *Bearish*: If price is below the Tenkan Sen (Figure 1.7).
- The Tenkan Sen should be pointing in the *same direction* as the trend. The steeper the angle, the greater the trend. In Figure 1.8, the Tenkan Sen is pointing upward with a steep angle. This is showing that the instrument is in a strong bullish (upward) trend.

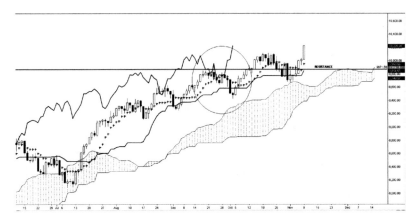

FIGURE 1.6   TradeStation Daily Ichimoku Chart of Feeder Cattle Nov 9, 2009

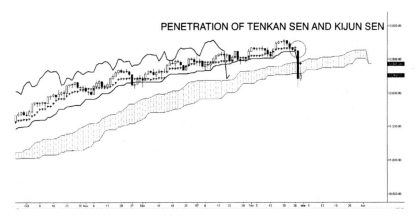

FIGURE 1.7   TradeStation Daily Ichimoku Chart of BBD Nov 9, 2009

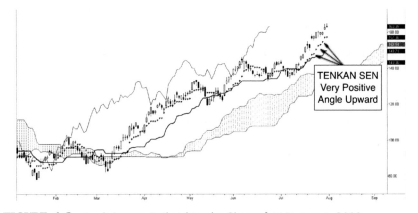

FIGURE 1.8   TradeStation Daily Ichimoku Chart of AAPL Aug 1, 2009

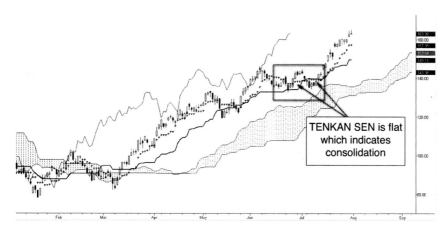

FIGURE 1.9 TradeStation Daily Ichimoku Chart of AAPL Aug 1, 2009

- If the Tenkan Sen is flat then it indicates that price *may* consolidate in the short term. If you are in a trade that is open then you should proceed with caution because the short-term trend could reverse soon (Figure 1.9).
- Tenkan Sen is a short-term support/resistance value. When price crosses the Tenkan Sen it is a major accomplishment because it has broken a major short-term support/resistance value (Figure 1.10).
- During a trend, if price crosses the Tenkan Sen in the opposite direction of the trend, it can indicate one of three different scenarios.
  - Minor Short-Term Pullback: A minor pullback is where price crosses over the Tenkan Sen but never crosses over the Kijun Sen. After it

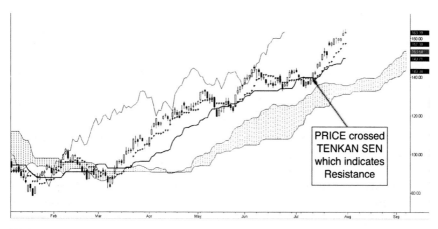

FIGURE 1.10 TradeStation Daily Ichimoku Chart of AAPL Aug 1, 2009

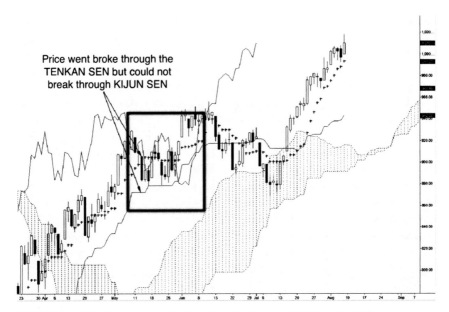

Price went broke through the
TENKAN SEN but could not
break through KIJUN SEN

FIGURE 1.11 TradeStation Daily Ichimoku Chart of SPX Aug 7, 2009

crosses the Tenkan Sen, price then continues on the original path
of the trend (Figure 1.11). This normally happens when short-term
traders take profit. The long-term traders continue to hold their current positions.

- Major Short-Term Pullback: A major pullback will have price crossing both the Tenkan Sen and Kijun Sen in the opposite direction of
  the trend. Once it has done that, price eventually continues on the
  original trend crossing back over both of them again (Figure 1.12).
  In this scenario, long-term position traders are taking *some* profits.
  They are not closing out their entire position at all because they believe the instrument will continue the trend after the major pullback
  has finished.

- Countertrend: The third scenario is similar to the second scenario
  where price crosses over both the Tenkan Sen and the Kijun Sen. The
  crossover takes place in the opposite direction of the trend. However, the major trend never resumes. Either the instrument enters a
  consolidation pattern (sideways) or a new trend forms (Figure 1.13).
  In this scenario, the long-term traders are exiting their positions completely. They can do so over a certain time period or all at once in
  some cases.

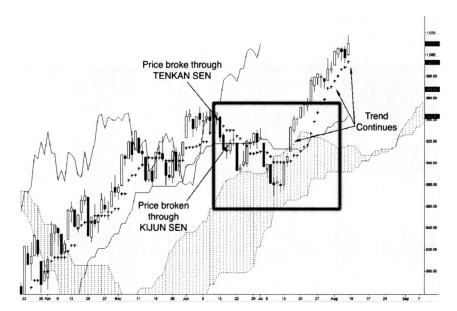

FIGURE 1.12 TradeStation Daily Ichimoku Chart of SPX Aug 7, 2009

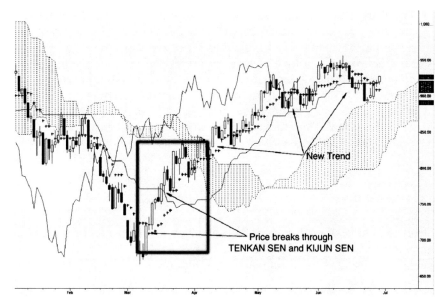

FIGURE 1.13 TradeStation Daily Ichimoku Chart of SPX June 29, 2009

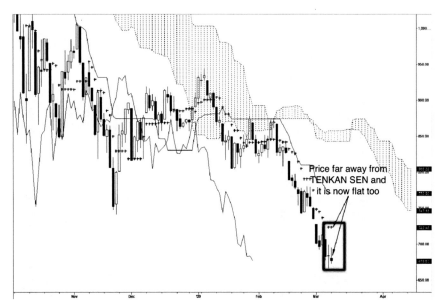

FIGURE 1.14 TradeStation Daily Ichimoku Chart of SPX March 9, 2009

- The Tenkan Sen should be *close* to price. If price and the Tenkan Sen are close to each other then the trend has been developing slowly without much interference from volatility. If price escapes from the Tenkan Sen then there is a high chance that price will pull back and try to go meet the Tenkan Sen because it was out of equilibrium too much. Figure 1.14 is a good illustration of this scenario. Sometimes, price may even go all the way to the Kijun Sen and past it for a major pullback or a trend reversal. Therefore, you have to be *careful* when price is out of equilibrium with Tenkan Sen.

KIJUN SEN

The second indicator I discuss is the Kijun Sen. It represents the medium-term movement for price. Therefore, it caters to a majority of the traders in the market. The color that represents the Kijun Sen is green. The formula for the Kijun Sen is:

$$\frac{(\text{Highest High} + \text{Lowest Low})}{2} \text{ for 26 periods}$$

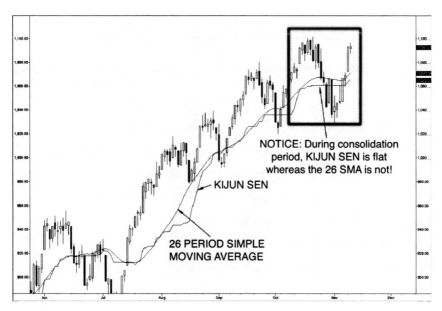

FIGURE 1.15 TradeStation Daily Ichimoku Chart of SPX Nov 9, 2009

The Kijun Sen is similar to the 30 period simple moving average that most retail and institution traders use (Figure 1.15). Just like the Tenkan Sen, the Kijun Sen is based on the Highest High and the Lowest Low. Instead of the 9 period of the Tenkan Sen, the Kijun Sen is based on 26 periods. For a daily time frame, the Kijun Sen roughly represents one month (and one trading week and one trading day) of history where the Tenkan Sen represented roughly $1^1/_2$ weeks (not including weekends on the chart). This is assuming I am not counting the weekends.

The Kijun Sen is one of the key indicators for the Ichimoku system. Many Ichimoku strategies focus around this one indicator. Here are the things to note about the Kijun Sen:

- Sentiment
  - *Bullish*: If price is above the Kijun Sen (Figure 1.16).
  - *Bearish*: If price is below the Kijun Sen (Figure 1.17).
- The Kijun Sen should be pointing in the same direction as the trend. The steeper the angle, the greater the trend. In Figure 1.18, the Kijun Sen was flat and then started to move upward. The Kijun Sen only moved up when the current price was higher than the average of the Highest High and the Lowest Low for the last 26 days. Unlike the Tenkan Sen, price has to move a lot in order to influence the Kijun Sen.

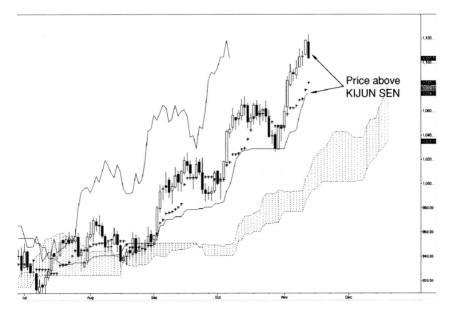

FIGURE 1.16 TradeStation Daily Ichimoku Chart of Mini Gold Futures
Nov 10, 2009

FIGURE 1.17 TradeStation Daily Ichimoku Chart of USDJPY Nov 11, 2009

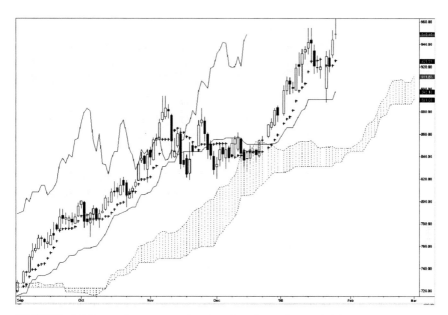

FIGURE 1.18 TradeStation Daily Ichimoku Chart of Mini Gold Futures
Jan 25, 2008

In using the Kijun Sen, we know that the trend has to be a minimum
26 days *established.* What does this mean? Will we miss the beginning
of the trend? The answer to that question is yes. We will definitely miss
the beginning of the trend because we are *waiting* for the trend to
establish itself. Why take a risk if price has not proven itself to us that
a trend can exist? If we get into a trade that is not in a trend then it is
in consolidation. With consolidation, your account will swing positive
and negative and back and forth.

- When the Kijun Sen is flat, it indicates that the price is consolidating
  and not trending (Figure 1.19).
- The Kijun Sen is a key support/resistance value. When price crosses
  the Kijun Sen, it is a major accomplishment because it broke a major
  support/resistance value (Figure 1.19).
- When price crosses the Kijun Sen, it indicates that a trend change *may*
  occur. This is key to determine if a major pullback or a trend reversal
  is about to occur. Neither one of them can occur until price crosses
  over the Kijun Sen (Figure 1.19).
- With price crossing over the Kijun Sen, one of two possible scenarios
  can occur:
  - Minor pullback: Price will bounce off the Kijun Sen and continue
    on the original trend path. Some people took profit but the major

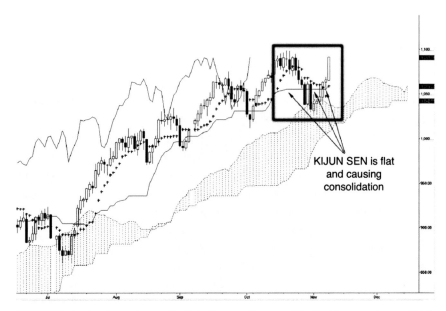

FIGURE 1.19   TradeStation Daily Ichimoku Chart of S&P Mini Futures Nov 9, 2009

"players" are still holding their positions and possibly increasing them now with the minor pullback. People really believe that the trend will continue strong (Figure 1.20).

- Major pullback: Price will cross over the Kijun Sen and eventually cross back to continue the major trend that was occurring (Figure 1.21). Long-term traders gained some profits but they still have some open positions because they believe the instrument will continue to move in the direction of the trend.

- Trend reversal: Price crosses the Kijun Sen once and then never crosses back over the Kijun Sen to continue the major trend. Instead, the instrument will enter a consolidation period or a trend reversal (Figure 1.22). The majority of the long-term traders are exiting their positions.

- The Kijun Sen should be *close* to price. When price is far away from the Kijun Sen it shows that price has moved at a faster rate than the Kijun Sen (Figure 1.23). A good trend has price and the Kijun Sen moving at a constant rate. Since the Kijun Sen represents 26 days, there is a high probability that price will retract toward the Kijun Sen causing a major *pullback or even a trend reversal.*

So how far is far considering the Kijun Sen is based on 26 periods? To determine what is "far," you can look back in time (history, previous bars)

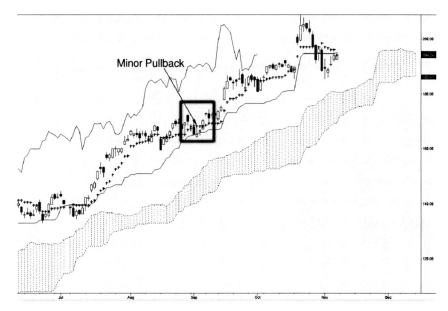

FIGURE 1.20 TradeStation Daily Ichimoku Chart of AAPL Nov 6, 2009

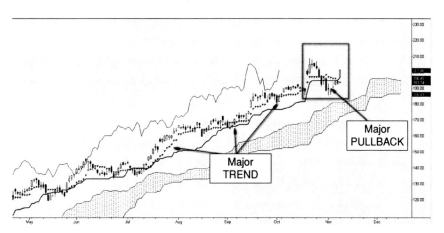

FIGURE 1.21 TradeStation Daily Ichimoku Chart of AAPL Nov 9, 2009

at other major pullbacks and trend reversals and determine what is "far" for price versus the Kijun Sen. Figure 1.23 illustrates one example of how you look at historical charts to determine the value of "far." The problem with looking back historically for a definite value for "far" is that it varies with time. *During high volatility these values will be bigger than during low volatility.* Therefore, the "far" value needs to be adjusted with volatility.

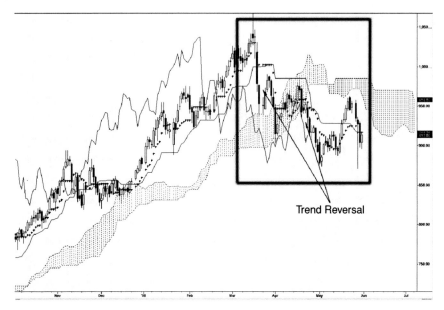

FIGURE 1.22 TradeStation Daily Ichimoku Chart of Mini Gold Future May 30, 2008

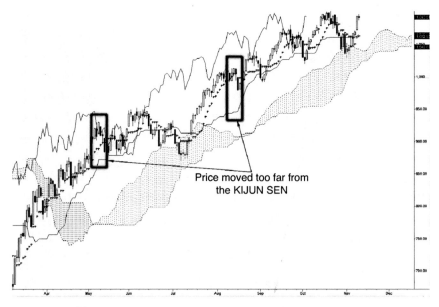

FIGURE 1.23 TradeStation Daily Ichimoku Chart of SPX Nov 9, 2009

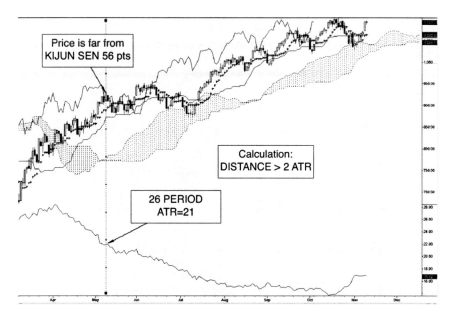

FIGURE 1.24 TradeStation Daily Ichimoku Chart of SPX Nov 9, 2009

Some traders use volatility indicators such as a multiple of Average True Range. Figure 1.24 shows how the price on June 8, 2009, was greater than 2×ATR and a pullback occurred. Therefore, one possible rule can be if price is greater than or equal to 1.5×ATR then price can be considered "far" away from Kijun Sen.

Let us look at one more example to understand the relationship of price and Kijun Sen. In Figure 1.25 you can see that price dropped and the bearish (downward) trend continued. When the trend continued, the Kijun Sen was pointing downward. Later, the Kijun Sen went flat, which indicated that price was consolidating. Since the Kijun Sen remained flat for a long period, it forced price and the Tenkan Sen to "meet it" instead of the Kijun Sen resuming its downward trend movement.

Up to this point, we have discussed the relationship of price and Tenkan Sen and then price and Kijun Sen. Now, let us put it all together to discuss the relationship among price, Tenkan Sen, and Kijun Sen. The analogy I like to use in my class to best illustrate the relationship among these three variables is where a couple is going for a walk in the park with their child. The couple's names are John and Mary and their son's name is Ben. Ben represents price, John represents the Kijun Sen, and Mary represents the Tenkan Sen. Initially, when the journey begins in the park, all three are together. They walk in the same direction together. Ben, like

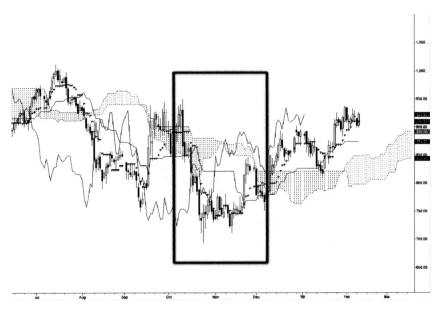

FIGURE 1.25 TradeStation Daily Ichimoku Chart of Mini Gold Futures
Feb 10, 2009

most children, tries continuously to walk faster than his parents. However, both Mary and John keep Ben in order and keep him close to them at all times. After some time, John gets an important phone call from work. When John receives the phone call, everyone is together. However, after some time, John starts to walk slower due to his phone call. As he walks slower, he begins to trail both Mary and Ben. Mary and Ben continue to walk at the normal pace so they are moving ahead of John gradually. They are doing that because the phone call conversation is disturbing the peaceful walk so they want some distance between John and themselves. As the phone call continues, John is further and further away from Mary and Ben. This creates some different scenarios for the walk. They are as follows.

The first scenario is where John makes a decision to continue to walk at a slow pace in hope of catching up with both Mary and Ben. However, as some time goes on, Mary and Ben will be so far ahead that they will not be able to see John anymore. This will pose a big problem because now Mary has to make some choices for herself. One choice is that both Mary and Ben stop and wait for John to catch up. This is assuming that John has not completely stopped walking. There is no way Mary knows that because John is not in viewing range anymore. Second, she can let Ben continue to walk a little further ahead of her while she walks slower in hope for John to catch up. If Ben gets too far from her, she will call out to him either to stop walking so she can catch up with him or she will call Ben to come to her. Once one of these two events occurs, Ben and Mary will have to wait for John to come. If he does not come after a long period of time, Mary will have to assume he has stopped walking completely so they will have to go back to find him. Once they find John, they have to make a decision on whether they want to continue to walk in the park or to go home.

The second scenario is where John makes a decision to stop walking completely due to the phone call. Mary sees that John has stopped walking but both Mary and Ben continue to walk forward. When they get to a point they cannot see John anymore, they will stop and return to where John had stopped walking.

These are just two of many different scenarios that can occur in this analogy. You should think of them all because this will give you a great insight on the relationship of price, Kijun Sen, and Tenkan Sen. You can take it one step further and associate the concept of pullbacks to the analogy, too.

CHIKOU SPAN

The third indicator I discuss is the Chikou Span (Figure 1.26). It represents the *momentum* of price. In other words, it tells you if a trend can occur or not occur. Remember, a trend is where price moves in one direction for a long period of time. The color that represents the Chikou Span is purple. The formula for the Chikou Span is:

Current Price Shifted back 26 periods

Simple as it sounds, it is the indicator that most people cannot understand. Also, it is one of my favorite Ichimoku indicators. Basically, it is today's price shifted back 26 periods. You compare today's price movements to price from 26 periods ago (Figure 1.27).

Here are the things to note about the Chikou Span:

- Sentiment
  - *Bullish*: If the Chikou Span is above price from 26 periods ago (Figure 1.28).
  - *Bearish*: If the Chikou Span is below price from 26 periods ago (Figure 1.29).

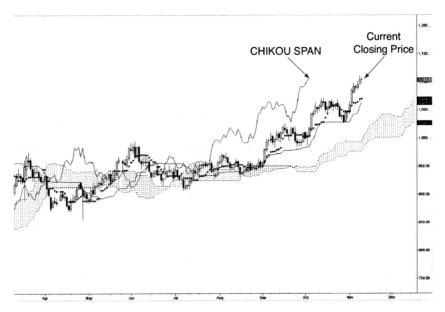

FIGURE 1.26   TradeStation Daily Ichimoku Chart of Mini Gold Futures
Nov 10, 2009

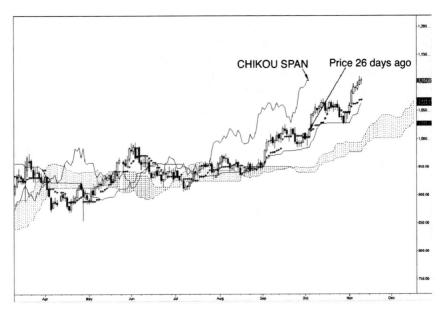

FIGURE 1.27   TradeStation Daily Ichimoku Chart of Mini Gold Futures
Nov 10, 2009

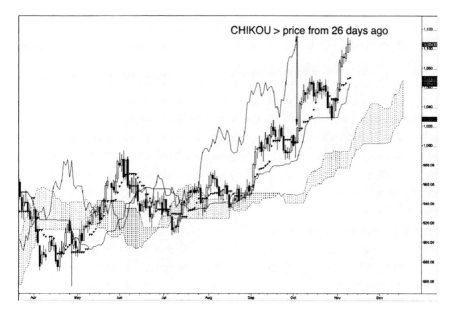

FIGURE 1.28　TradeStation Daily Ichimoku Chart of Mini Gold Futures
Nov 10, 2009

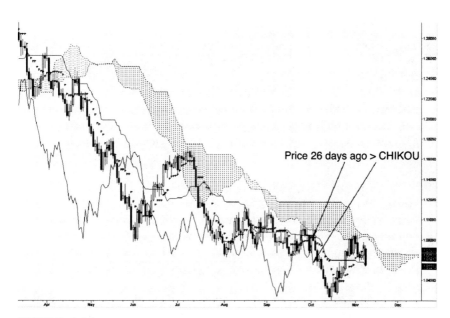

FIGURE 1.29　TradeStation Daily Ichimoku Chart of USDCAD Nov 9, 2009

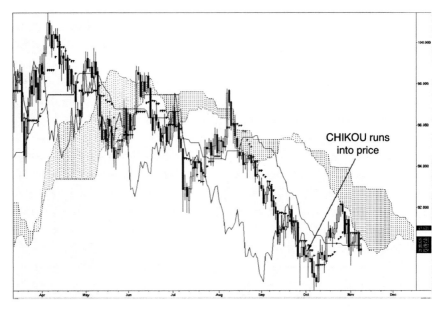

FIGURE 1.30 TradeStation Daily Ichimoku Chart of USDJPY Nov 9, 2009

- *Consolidation*: If the Chikou Span is touching or very close to price from 26 periods ago (Figure 1.30).
- This indicator is a momentum indicator. The way you judge momentum is to determine if the Chikou Span is going to run into price in the next couple of periods. I typically look ahead 5 to 10 periods. If the Chikou Span runs into price, then there is not much of a trend momentum. Price action in the past represents support/resistance in the future, which causes major problems for current trends. If the Chikou Span is in "open space" then the trend momentum is strong because today's price is not going to run into any price support/resistance from 26 periods ago.

Figure 1.31 illustrates a good example where the momentum is strong. The Chikou Span is below price from 26 days ago so it is bearish. If price consolidates for a couple of days, the Chikou still will *not* run into price. The Chikou is in "open white space" where only a big drastic movement can cause it to run into price. Therefore it is strong bearish, which means that there is a high probability of a bearish trend occurring or continuing.

Figure 1.32 illustrates an example of where the Chikou Span has weak momentum. Based on what happens in the next couple of days,

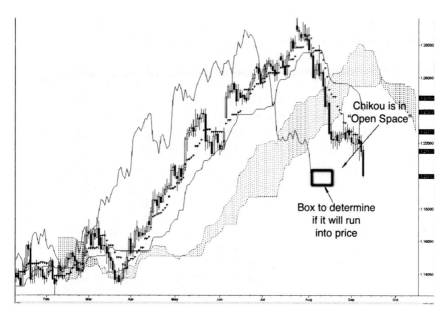

FIGURE 1.31 TradeStation Daily Ichimoku Chart of AUDNZD Sept 9, 2008

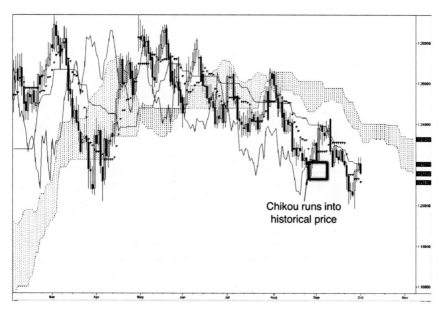

FIGURE 1.32 TradeStation Daily Ichimoku Chart of AUDNZD Sept 29, 2009

the Chikou Span could become bullish (trend reversal) or consolidate for momentum, two scenarios that are not good when you are looking at trading a bearish trend.

When you judge the momentum based on the Chikou Span for an instrument, you have to look vertically and horizontally on when the Chikou could run into price. If price moves up or down 5 percent to 10 percent, will it run into price? If price consolidates for 5 or 10 trading days, will it run into price? Some of my students actually create a visual square box after the Chikou Span. If price hits that box then the momentum is very weak. Go through the various scenarios in your mind to see what could happen. Figure 1.33 illustrates a "visual box" around the Chikou Span for the AUDNZD currency on Nov 9, 2009.

- The Chikou peaks are major support and resistance values. If you draw a horizontal line through a Chikou peak, it represents a support/resistance value. If you get many Chikou peaks hitting that horizontal line then it is a major support/resistance value. In most cases, if you get two or more peaks, this typically represents a Fibonacci value.

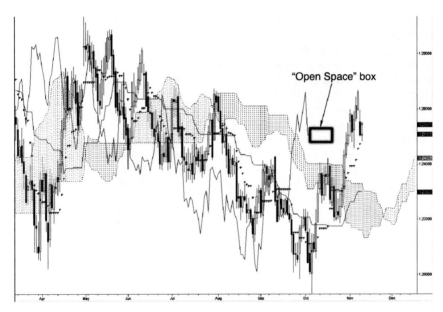

FIGURE 1.33 TradeStation Daily Ichimoku Chart of AUDNZD Nov 9, 2009

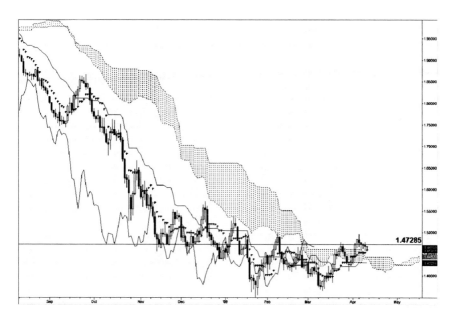

FIGURE 1.34   TradeStation Daily Ichimoku Chart of GBPUSD Apr 10, 2009

Figure 1.34 shows a horizontal line drawn where it intersects five Chikou peaks.

Figure 1.35 shows the same chart as Figure 1.34, but now we have overlaid the Fibonacci values on top of the chart. Notice the Fibonacci value of 23.60 percent retracement matches the support/resistance line drawn from the Chikou Span. This is just one example of how other indicators are "built in" Ichimoku Kinko Hyo.

KUMO CLOUD COMPONENTS

The last two indicators remaining are the Senkou Span A and Senkou Span B (Figure 1.36). These are discussed differently from that of the other Ichimoku indicators. The reason is that together they provide a lot of information. Together, they form a cloud called the "Kumo Cloud." The Cloud is formed by filling the gap between the Senkou Span A and Senkou Span B with a particular color. If Senkou A is greater than Senkou B then the color is yellow (bullish) and if Senkou A is less than Senkou B then the color is red (bearish). You can use any color for the Kumo Cloud, but this is the color I like to use on my charts (Figure 1.37).

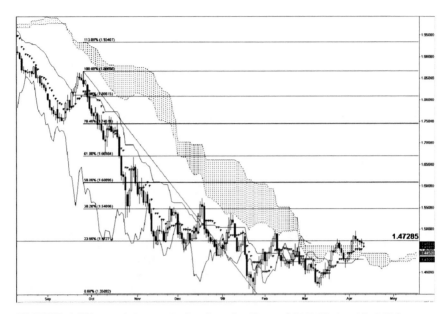

FIGURE 1.35 TradeStation Daily Ichimoku Chart of GBPUSD Apr 10, 2009

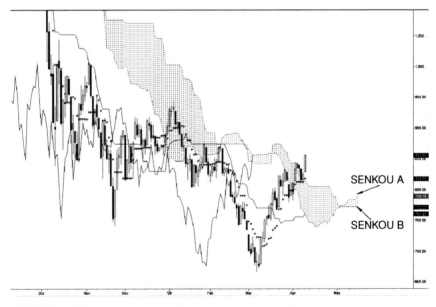

FIGURE 1.36 TradeStation Daily Ichimoku Chart of SPX Apr 9, 2009

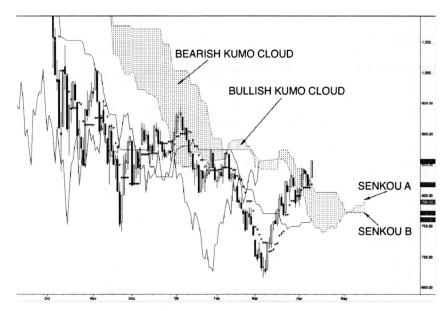

FIGURE 1.37 TradeStation Daily Ichimoku Chart of SPX Apr 9, 2009

In this section, I reference two types of clouds:

1. Kumo Cloud: Cloud above/below current price (Figure 1.38).
2. Future Kumo Cloud: Cloud 26 bars into the future (Figure 1.38).

SENKOU SPAN A

The fourth indicator I discuss is the Senkou A. This represents half of the "Kumo Cloud," which I discuss later. The color that represents the Senkou A is dark blue. The formula for the Senkou A is:

$$\frac{(\text{Tenkan Sen} + \text{Kijun Sen})}{2} \text{ Shifted forward in time 26 periods}$$

This indicator confuses most people because there are really two Kumo Clouds, the current Kumo Cloud and the Future Kumo Cloud. You have to look at two Senkou A, the current one and the future Senkou A. The current Senkou A is the average of the Tenkan Sen and Kijun Sen *from* 26 periods ago. Therefore, when you compare the current price against Senkou A, you are really comparing current price to the Tenkan/Kijun Sen

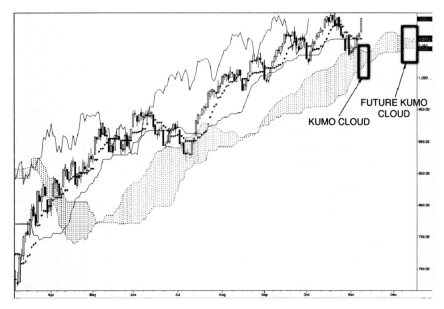

FIGURE 1.38   TradeStation Daily Ichimoku Chart of SPX Nov 9, 2009

values from 26 periods ago. The future Senkou A is the average of the *current* Tenkan Sen and the *current* Kijun Sen (Figure 1.39). Current price movement will influence the future.

SENKOU SPAN B

The fifth indicator I discuss is the Senkou B. This represents the second half of the "Kumo Cloud," which I discuss later. The color that represents the Senkou B is purple. The formula for the Senkou B is:

$$\frac{(\text{Highest High} + \text{Lowest Low})}{2} \quad \text{for 52 periods and then shifted forward by 26 periods}$$

This indicator deals with 52 periods, the most periods out of all the Ichimoku indicators. For a weekly time frame, this is 52 weeks. Remember, we have two Senkou Bs just like Senkou A. The Senkou B is really the calculation from 52 periods ago. The future Senkou B is the current calculation. This is powerful because the Senkou B incorporates many historical bars (Figure 1.40).

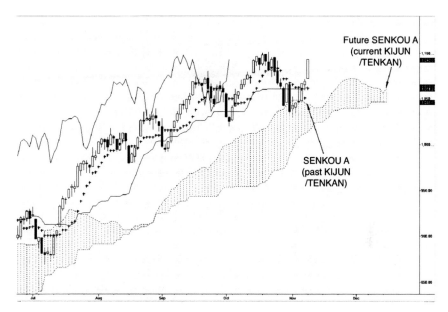

FIGURE 1.39 TradeStation Daily Ichimoku Chart of SPX Nov 9, 2009

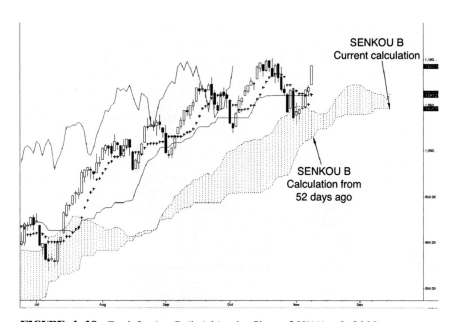

FIGURE 1.40 TradeStation Daily Ichimoku Chart of SPX Nov 9, 2009

KUMO CLOUD

Here are the things to note about the Kumo Cloud:

- Current Sentiment:
  - *Bullish*: Price is above the Kumo Cloud (Figure 1.41).
  - *Bearish*: Price is below the Kumo Cloud (Figure 1.42).
  - *Consolidation*: Price is within the Kumo Cloud (Figure 1.43).
- Future Sentiment (Future Senkou A and Senkou B):
  - *Bullish*: Senkou A is above Senkou B (Figure 1.44).
  - *Bearish*: Senkou A is below Senkou B (Figure 1.45).
  - *Consolidation*: Senkou A is equal to Senkou B (Figure 1.46).
- Strength: The strength of the Future Kumo Cloud is determined by both the future Senkou A and future Senkou B. Here are the different scenarios:
  - *Strong Bullish*: Kumo Future is bullish and both future Senkou A and future Senkou B are pointing upward (trend) (Figure 1.47).
  - *Medium Bullish*: Future Kumo Future is bullish, future Senkou A is pointing upward, and future Senkou B is flat (Figure 1.48).
  - *Weak Bullish*: Future Kumo Future is bullish, future Senkou A is pointing downward, and future Senkou B is flat. In other words, this can be a major pullback or a trend reversal (Figure 1.49).

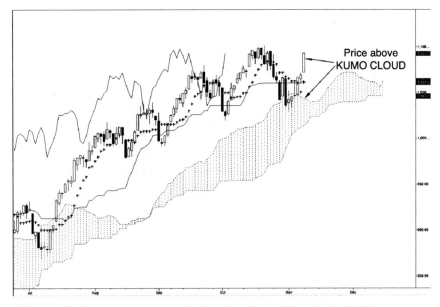

FIGURE 1.41 TradeStation Daily Ichimoku Chart of SPX Nov 9, 2009

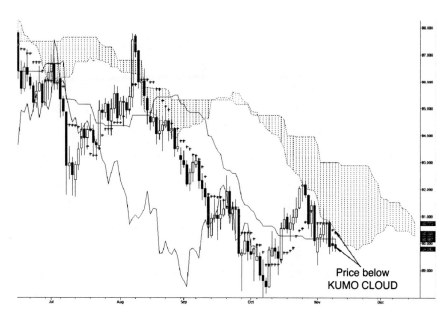

FIGURE 1.42 TradeStation Daily Ichimoku Chart of USDJPY Nov 9, 2009

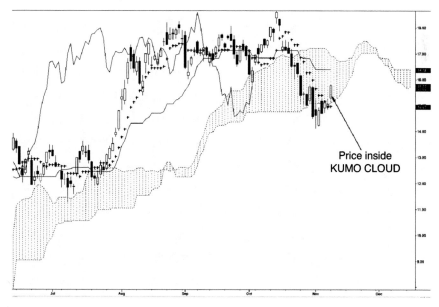

FIGURE 1.43 TradeStation Daily Ichimoku Chart of BAC Nov 9, 2009

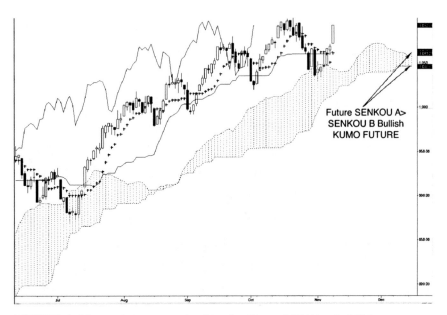

FIGURE 1.44 TradeStation Daily Ichimoku Chart of SPX Nov 9, 2009

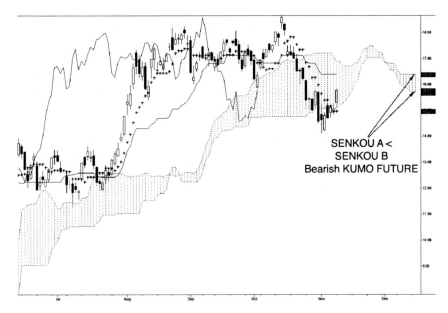

FIGURE 1.45 TradeStation Daily Ichimoku Chart of BAC Nov 9, 2009

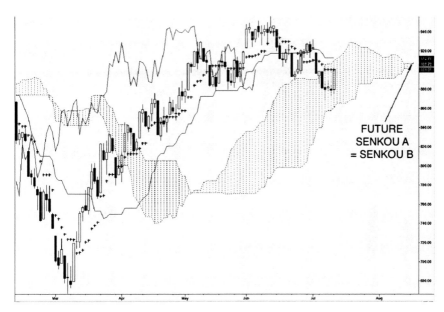

FIGURE 1.46 TradeStation Daily Ichimoku Chart of SPX July 13, 2009

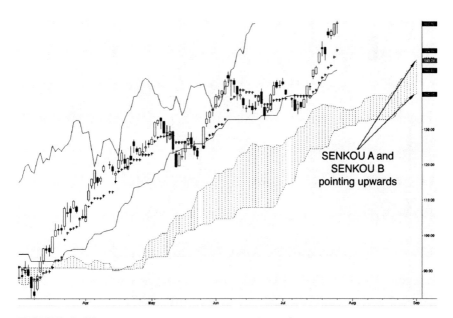

FIGURE 1.47 TradeStation Daily Ichimoku Chart of AAPL July 27, 2009

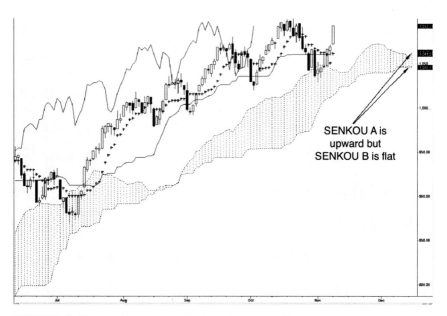

FIGURE 1.48   TradeStation Daily Ichimoku Chart of SPX Nov 9, 2009

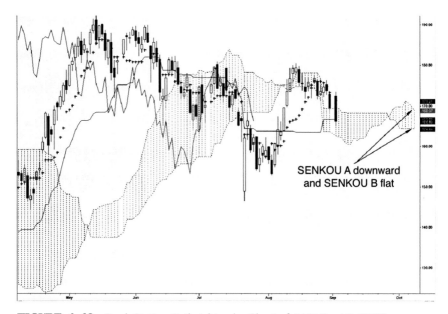

FIGURE 1.49   TradeStation Daily Ichimoku Chart of AAPL Sept 2, 2008

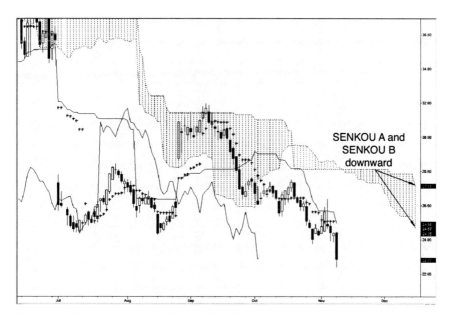

FIGURE 1.50 TradeStation Daily Ichimoku Chart of MYGN Nov 9, 2009

- *Strong Bearish*: Future Kumo Future is bearish and both future Senkou A and future Senkou B are pointing downward (trend) (Figure 1.50).
- *Medium Bearish*: Future Kumo Future is bearish, future Senkou A is pointing downward, and future Senkou B is flat. This means that there is minor pullback or major pullback with high volatility (Figure 1.51).
- *Weak Bearish*: Future Kumo Future is bearish, future Senkou A is pointing downward, and future Senkou B is flat. This means that there is a major pullback or trend reversal (Figure 1.52).
- Kumo shadow represents major support and resistance values. A Kumo shadow is a cloud that exists *behind* price. They are created from past consolidation patterns and trend reversals (Figure 1.53).

Figure 1.54 shows a Kumo shadow for a price movement going up (bullish). Until price moves above the Kumo shadow, it will run into resistance causing it to consolidate. If price consolidates for a while then the shadow will get weaker and weaker. The closer the shadow is to current price, the stronger it is in influencing price. Therefore, a *strong* trend really cannot occur until it breaks through the price of the peak of the shadow. The shadows were created from past price consolidations, which are now current support and resistance values.

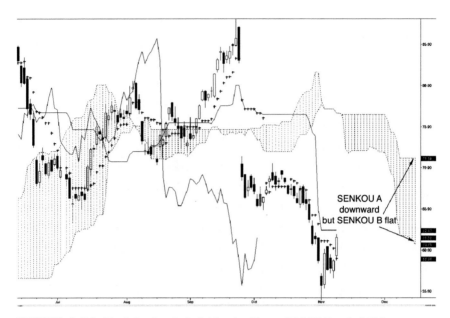

FIGURE 1.51 TradeStation Daily Ichimoku Chart of RIMM Nov 9, 2009

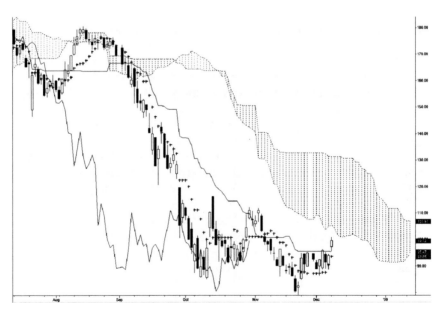

FIGURE 1.52 TradeStation Daily Ichimoku Chart of AAPL Dec 8, 2008

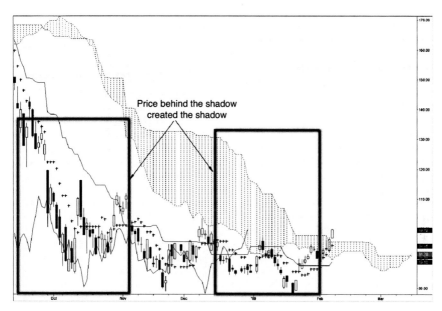

FIGURE 1.53 TradeStation Daily Ichimoku Chart of AAPL Feb 6, 2009

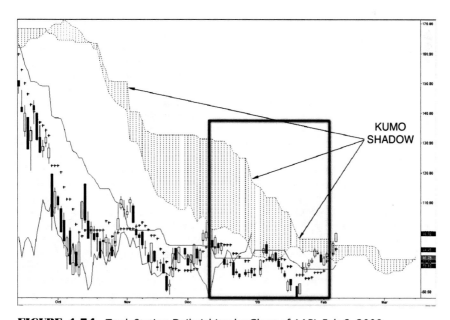

FIGURE 1.54 TradeStation Daily Ichimoku Chart of AAPL Feb 6, 2009

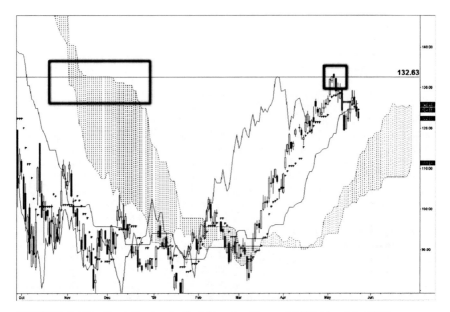

FIGURE 1.55 TradeStation Daily Ichimoku Chart of AAPL May 21, 2009

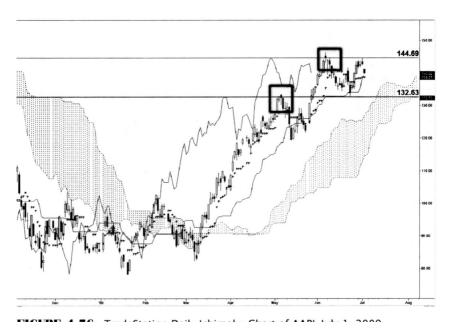

FIGURE 1.56 TradeStation Daily Ichimoku Chart of AAPL July 1, 2009

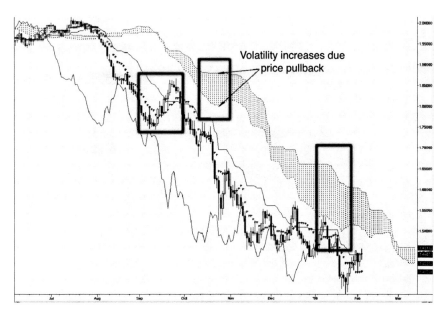

FIGURE 1.57 TradeStation Daily Ichimoku Chart of GBPUSD Feb 2, 2009

- The flat Senkou B of the Kumo Cloud is a major support and resistance value. The longer the flat part of Senkou B, the greater the support/resistance value it is going to be to cause problems for the current or future trend. In Figure 1.55, price just penetrated barely above the Senkou B (past) resistance of the Kumo Cloud (shadow). Notice how flat the Senkou was in the past around that price range. It acts as a major resistance to a point and it caused a major pullback in the bullish trend action.
- The peaks created by Senkou A of the Kumo Cloud are a major support and resistance value (Figure 1.56).

   The spacing between Senkou A and Senkou B for the future Kumo Cloud represents volatility. The thicker the future cloud, the more consolidation has occurred. This in turn causes high volatility. When a *major* trend occurs, the future Kumo Cloud will be thin with both Senkou A and Senkou B pointing in the direction of the Kumo Cloud (Figure 1.57).

## CHAPTER 2

Ichimoku Trading Plan

I n this section, the Ichimoku trading plan will be created. Once this trading plan has been created, it will be backtested in the next section to see whether it is historically successful. It is understood that past results do not always reflect future results. However, if the backtest results are successful, there is a high probability that future results may be successful as well.

COMPONENTS

The trading plan we use for our trading is listed later. I have created a simple trading plan; however, you can change anything in *your* trading plan. Everyone is different and has a different style of trading. Therefore, the trading plan should fit your style of trading. If you do not know your style, you need to paper-trade various trading plans until you can determine your trading style. *Do not* trade until you know your strengths and weaknesses when it comes to trading.

Also, *do not* trade without having a trading plan written down. Would you start a business without a business plan? You have to think and *act* like it is a business in order to *succeed*. If not, you will fail.

Here is our trading plan:

- We only trade currencies. We never trade more than four currencies at one time because it is hard to manage more than four currencies at one time.
- We never allocate more than 20 percent of my funds at one time.
- Margin is *not* used.
- No Add-ons, which means that once a trade is entered, more positions cannot be added.
- Only instruments that show a positive backtest result can be traded. If backtesting for an instrument has not been done, then that instrument *cannot* be traded live.
- No decision making is made at all. The trading plan is followed with no exceptions.
- All trades are evaluated on a monthly basis to determine if the trading plan and/or strategy need to be changed.
- Only Daily time frame is used to trade.
- Only the Currency Spot Market is traded, which means that there are no currency options.
- An instrument is analyzed once and either Alerts or Entries are placed for both the bullish and the bearish side. We do not look at that instrument again until an Alert/Entry is triggered. All Alerts are readjusted on a weekly basis.
- Always place Alerts below resistance values and above major support values so that an entry can be placed before the major action occurs.

STRATEGY DESCRIPTION

In this section, we concentrate on currency trading. The current strategy can easily be changed and be adopted for stocks, futures, bonds, and so forth. Ichimoku works for all instruments. Remember, *each* instrument has its own characteristics; therefore you may have a different strategy for individual or groups of instruments. For example, the exit/entry buffer for the instrument EURUSD (Europe currency versus United States currency) can be different from GBPUSD (Great Britain currency versus United States currency) because EURUSD can be less volatile than the GBPUSD. If you use a hard-core value, then for the EURUSD you can have an entry/exit buffer of 40 pips, but for GBPUSD it would be 50 pips. Therefore, you have one strategy for EURUSD and one for GBPUSD. If you want to simplify, you can use Average True Range for the buffer and have one strategy for both currencies.

Bullish Strategy (Instrument Will Go Higher)

Entry Rules	Rules
	Price has to be above Kumo Cloud
	Tenkan Sen is greater than Kijun Sen
	Chikou is showing strong bullish momentum ("Open Space")
	There should be at least 50 pips to the next *major* support or resistance value
	Kumo Future is bullish
	Entry Price has to be less than 200 pips from the Tenkan Sen. If not, you have to wait for it to equalize and come back into range
	Entry Price has to be less than 300 pips from the Kijun Sen. If not, you have to wait for it to equalize and come back into range
	Entry buffers equals 40 pips
	All Ichimoku Indicators have to be Bullish
Money Management	
	If price is greater than 200 pips from TS, exit if TS is *flat*
	If profit is equal or greater than 300 pips, use TS with buffer as your stop
	Exit Buffer equals 40 pips
	Place/adjust Bullish Alert
	Adjust stops every day
	Place alert at Kijun Sen to cancel Entry orders

Bearish Strategy (Instrument Will Go Higher)

Entry Rules	Rules
	Price has to be below Kumo Cloud
	Tenkan Sen is less than Kijun Sen
	Chikou is showing strong bearish momentum ("Open Space")
	There should be at least 50 pips to the next *major* support or resistance value
	Kumo Future is bearish
	Entry Price has to be less than 200 pips from the Tenkan Sen. If not, you have to wait for it to equalize and come back into range
	Entry Price has to be less than 300 pips from the Kijun Sen. If not, you have to wait for it to equalize and come back into range
	Entry buffers equals 35 pips
	All Ichimoku Indicators have to be Bearish
Money Management	
	If price is greater than 200 pips from TS, exit if TS is *flat*
	If profit is equal or greater than 250 pips, use TS with buffer as your stop
	Exit Buffer equals 35 pips
	Place/adjust Bearish Alert
	Adjust stops every day
	Place alert at Kijun Sen to cancel Entry orders

## CHAPTER 3

Ichimoku
Backtesting

When someone meets a successful trader, what type of questions does he or she normally receive? How much profit do you make? How long have you been trading? What is your winning percentage for your system? Is this your only revenue source?

These are just a few of many questions that people ask over and over to successful traders. When inquiring about a system, do you think these are the first questions you should ask? When the trader provides the answers, are the answers *facts*? Can you believe everything the trader tells you? What good are the statistics for the trader's system if you do not know *how* that person trades? If you knew how that person trades then you can calculate the statistics yourself through backtesting.

BACKTESTING

Today there are many trading systems that offer various statistics on "how successful they are." The way to examine trading systems is not by looking at the winning trades but instead by looking at the losing trades. During a "bull run," anyone can create a system and it performs well. The person only has to be bullish over a long period. How will their system perform if the market all of a sudden reversed completely? Will there be a system loss to a point where it wipes out two years of profit? If you do not believe this can happen, search the Web on what happened in 2008 to many traders. Some traders lost four years of profits in three months!

When I first met my mentor, I did not ask him how much profit he makes in a week or a month. The first thing I asked him is how he trades. I listened over and over to obtain all the knowledge he had gained about trading with Ichimoku for years. After receiving some basic answers, I proceeded to validate what he had told me. Validation was achieved by backtesting his system over a certain time period with a targeted list of instruments. Once the backtesting was completed, I examined the results and instantly that person became my mentor.

My mentor did not understand the concept for backtesting so all the training I received was live. Also, it was targeted only at the currency market because that is all he knew. After a couple of months of mentoring in the "live" mode, I took all the knowledge that I gained from him and formulated various trading plans. These trading plans were then backtested with stocks, futures, currencies, bonds, and so forth. I literally backtested over six months. At the end of that journey, I took the trading plans that were successful in historical mode and started to trade them live. Historical trading is different from live trading. In live trading, all the emotions "kick in," which, in turn, can cause you to fail. Years later, I am still trading Ichimoku Kinko Hyo. In fact, I surpassed my mentor in that I use Ichimoku to trade *all* instruments and also have various trading plans and strategies for different market situations.

EURUSD—A TWO-YEAR BACKTEST

In this section, we take our trading plan with our strategy and backtest it for one instrument. We choose the EURUSD currency instrument and the backtest period from January 1, 2007, to November 9, 2009, a two-year backtest period (Figure 3.1).

The complete analysis of the Ichimoku indicators for January 1, 2007, follows.

- Price versus Kumo Cloud: Bullish (Figure 3.2).
- TS versus KS relationship: Bullish (Figure 3.3).
  - Distance from TS: $1.3272 - 1.3189 = 0.0083 = 83$ pips (within 200 pips specified in trading plan).
  - Distance from KS: $1.3272 - 1.3154 = 0.0118 = 118$ pips (within 300 pips specified in trading plan).
  - In Kumo Cloud: No (within a Kumo Cloud indicates consolidation).
  - Tenkan Sen Trend: Yes (pointing in bullish direction).
  - Kijun Sen Trend: Yes (slightly pointing in bullish direction and has not been flat for a long time).

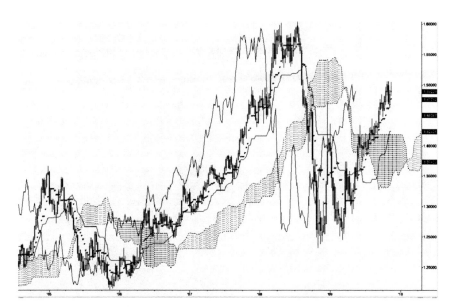

FIGURE 3.1 TradeStation Weekly Chart Daily of EURUSD from Jan 1, 2007, to Nov 9, 2009

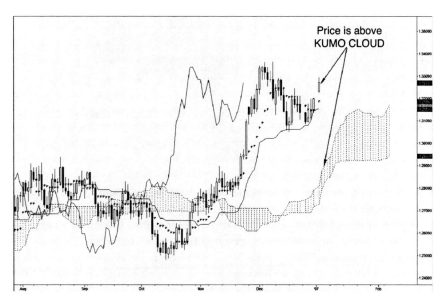

FIGURE 3.2 TradeStation Daily Ichimoku Chart of EURUSD Jan 1, 2007

FIGURE 3.3 TradeStation Daily Ichimoku Chart of EURUSD Jan 1, 2007

- Chikou: Bullish (above price from 26 days ago) (Figure 3.4).
  - Horizontal predication: Weak, can run into price if it consolidates for four or more days.
  - Vertical predication: Weak, a 100-pip movement down can make the Chikou touch price from 26 days ago.
  - Trending Criteria requirement: If price can clear the last ultimate high, which is less than 100 pips away, it has a chance to get into a strong "open area." In the "open area" the bullish trend can develop some momentum.
  - In Kumo Cloud: No: within a Kumo Cloud indicates consolidation.
- Kumo Cloud (Figure 3.5).
  - Future Cloud: Bullish.
  - Senkou A Trending: Yes: Pointing in direction of trend.
  - Senkou B Trending: Yes: Pointing in the direction of the trend.
  - Thickness of Future cloud: Thick: Indicates that the trend *may* not be a long-term trend, more medium- to short-term trend.
  - Kumo Shadows: No: within 12-month period.

The analysis shows that all the indicators are bullish. What if price was removed from the chart as shown in Figure 3.6, can you tell from the Ichimoku indicators what has happened to price over time? The answer is yes. You can clearly see what happened to price. If you cannot see that,

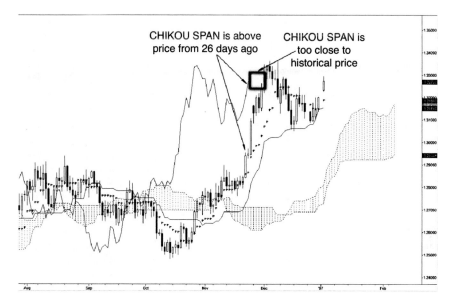

FIGURE 3.4 TradeStation Daily Ichimoku Chart of EURUSD Jan 1, 2007

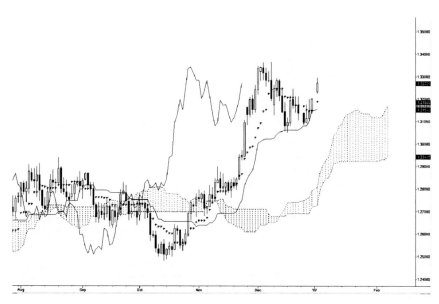

FIGURE 3.5 TradeStation Daily Ichimoku Chart of EURUSD Jan 1, 2007

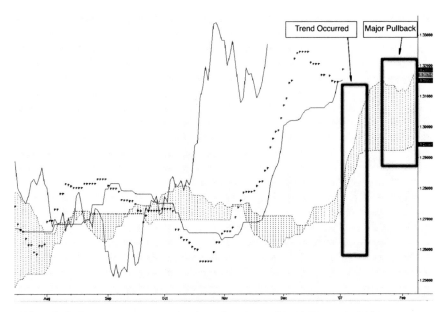

FIGURE 3.6 TradeStation Daily Ichimoku Chart of EURUSD Jan 1, 2007

you will once you practice more at looking at Ichimoku Kinko Hyo charts. The best way, believe it or not, is to remove price from the chart and examine the chart. The future Kumo Cloud indicates that a trend has developed already and that we are looking at a continuation trend due to the thickness of the Kumo Cloud and the future Senkou A pointing upward. Also, the Chikou is telling us that we should not enter unless price reaches our bullish alert (close to the ultimate high seen on the chart) where it has a chance to gain momentum.

Action: We are going to place our bullish and bearish alerts and wait for those alerts to trigger (Figure 3.7). The bearish alert can be placed either below the Kijun Sen (indicates a trend change) or at the Kumo Cloud. I have chosen the Kumo Cloud for the bearish alert because the Kumo Cloud is thick. If the Kumo Cloud were thin, I would have chosen the alert to be below the Kijun Sen since it could go right through a thin Kumo Cloud.

For the bullish alert, I looked at the highest Chikou peak and placed an alert below that peak. Remember, the Chikou Span represents the *closing* price shifted back 26 periods, not the highest price shifted 26 periods ago. If we put an alert below the highest peak in the Chikou Span line then we have a chance to place an entry trade before the last high is exceeded. Remember, you do not want to miss the opportunity because if

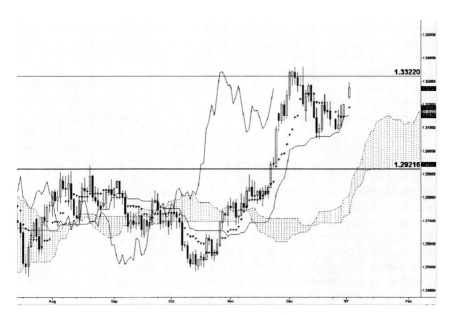

FIGURE 3.7 TradeStation Daily Ichimoku Chart of EURUSD Jan 1, 2007

you do, you will have to wait for the next trade, which may not be for a while.

The bearish alert was triggered on January 11, 2007, as illustrated in Figure 3.8. The complete analysis of the Ichimoku indicators for this day follows:

- Price versus Kumo Cloud: Bearish: The closing price is below Kumo Cloud as illustrated in Figure 3.9.
- TS versus KS relationship: Bearish (Figure 3.10).
  - Distance from TS: 1.3088 – 1.2891 = 0.0097 = 97 pips (within 200 pips specified in trading plan).
  - Distance from KS: 1.3123 – 1.2891 = 0.0232 = 232 pips (within 300 pips specified in trading plan).
  - In Kumo Cloud: No, but will be soon. It is a thick cloud.
  - Tenkan Sen Trend: Yes: Pointing in the bearish direction.
  - Kijun Sen Trend: Yes: Pointing in the bearish direction.
- Chikou: Bearish (below price from 26 days ago) (Figure 3.11).
  - Horizontal predication: Strong Bearish.
  - Vertical predication: Strong Bearish.
  - Trending Criteria requirement: It is in "open space" already.
  - In Kumo Cloud: No, within a Kumo Cloud indicates consolidation.

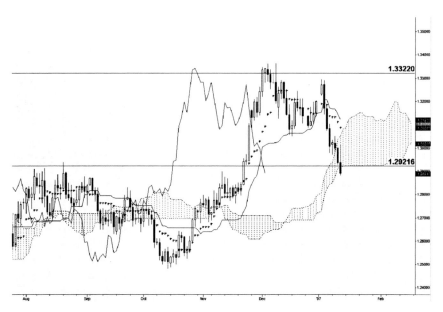

FIGURE 3.8   TradeStation Daily Ichimoku Chart of EURUSD Jan 11, 2007

FIGURE 3.9   TradeStation Daily Ichimoku Chart of EURUSD Jan 11, 2007

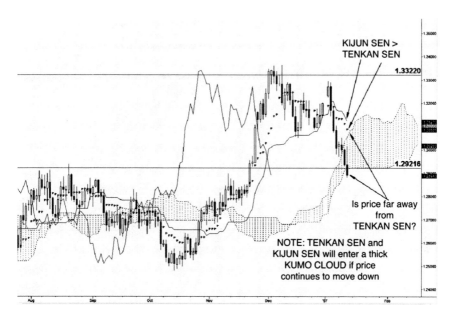

FIGURE 3.10 TradeStation Daily Ichimoku Chart of EURUSD Jan 11, 2007

FIGURE 3.11 TradeStation Daily Ichimoku Chart of EURUSD Jan 11, 2007

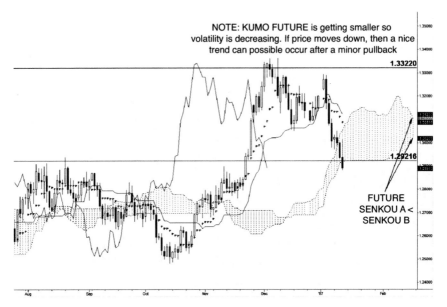

FIGURE 3.12   TradeStation Daily Ichimoku Chart of EURUSD Jan 11, 2007

- Kumo Cloud (Figure 3.12).
  - Future Cloud: Bullish
  - Senkou A Trending: No: Pointing in opposite direction of trend.
  - Senkou B Trending: Yes, slightly pointing up still.
  - Thickness of Future Cloud: Future Kumo Cloud is thinning now with Senkou A moving down to meet Senkou B. Either we are in a major pullback or a trend reversal.
- Kumo Shadows: No, within 12-month period.

Action: At this time, there is conflict among the indicators. There-fore, we are going to reset our alerts (Figure 3.13). The Bearish alert will be moved *above* the next major support. If you are not sure where that lo-cation is choose a very conservative alert where you will get alerted right away on the next move down. Remember, it is better to be alerted a lot instead of missing the major move. For the bullish alert, we are going to move it to the top of the Kumo Cloud.

The bullish alert was triggered on February 26, 2007. Before we go through and perform the Ichimoku analysis for that day, did you notice the mistake we made earlier (Figure 3.14)? We violated the trading plan rule where alerts should be placed *below* the major resistance. The alert was placed at a major resistance, the top of the Kumo Cloud on January 11,

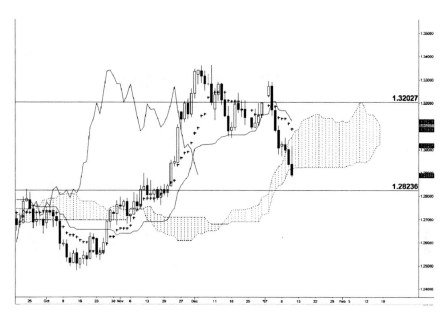

FIGURE 3.13 TradeStation Daily Ichimoku Chart of EURUSD Jan 11, 2007

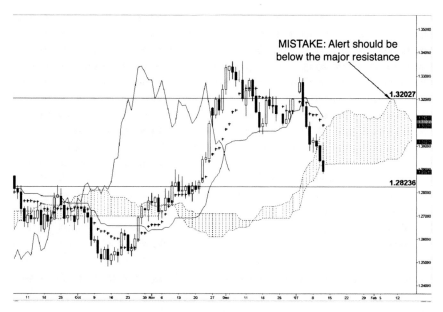

FIGURE 3.14 TradeStation Daily Ichimoku Chart of EURUSD Jan 11, 2007

FIGURE 3.15 TradeStation Daily Ichimoku Chart of EURUSD Jan 11, 2007

2007. Therefore, we should have placed an alert below the top of the Kumo Cloud. Pay close attention to details and *follow your trading plan*. If you caught the mistake, great job! Now, did you see why the alert is placed below the major resistance? If we place an alert below the major resistance when triggered, we would be in the perfect position to place an order entry to "play" the breakout of that major resistance. If the alert was at the major resistance, the breakout of the major resistance would have caused only the alert to trigger. At that point, we then can place an order entry.

Due to the mistake, we are going to "rewind" everything and do it *correctly*. Therefore, Figure 3.15 shows the correct alerts that should have been placed on January 11, 2007.

With the alerts corrected, we can now continue our backtesting. On February 20, 2007, our alert was triggered. Figure 3.16 shows the chart at this time.

Here is the Ichimoku analysis for the chart in Figure 3.16.

- Price versus Kumo Cloud: Bullish: Closed above the Kumo Cloud (Figure 3.17).
- TS versus KS relationship: Bullish (Figure 3.18).
  - Distance from TS: 1.3136 − 1.3065 = 0.0071 = 71 pips (within 200 pips specified in trading plan).

FIGURE 3.16 TradeStation Daily Ichimoku Chart of EURUSD Feb 20, 2007

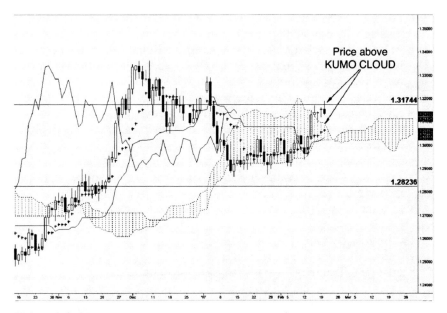

FIGURE 3.17 TradeStation Daily Ichimoku Chart of EURUSD Feb 20, 2007

FIGURE 3.18 TradeStation Daily Ichimoku Chart of EURUSD Feb 20, 2007

- Distance from KS: 1.3136 − 1.3033 = 0.0103 = 103 pips (within 300 pips specified in trading plan).
- In Kumo Cloud: Kijun Sen just entered the Kumo Cloud. However, if it moves up, it will exit the Kumo Cloud so we need a bullish move to get it out of the Kumo Cloud.
- TS Trend: Yes: Pointing in the bearish direction.
- KS Trend: Yes: Pointing in the bearish direction.
- Chikou: Bearish (below price from 26 days ago) (Figure 3.19).
  - Horizontal predication: Strong Bullish.
  - Vertical predication: Strong Bullish if price moves higher.
  - Trending Criteria requirement: It will be in "open space" if price moves higher.
  - In Kumo Cloud: No, but if price moves lower, it can be in the Kumo Cloud.
- Future Kumo Cloud (Figure 3.20).
  - Future Cloud: Bearish (turning).
  - Senkou A Trending: Yes: Pointing in bullish direction.
  - Senkou B Trending: No, staying flat so Senkou A can cross it and turn the Kumo future bullish.
  - Thickness of Future Cloud: Thin indicating that a trend can occur.
  - Kumo Shadows: Yes, but once price moves above the top of the Kumo Cloud there will be no more shadows.

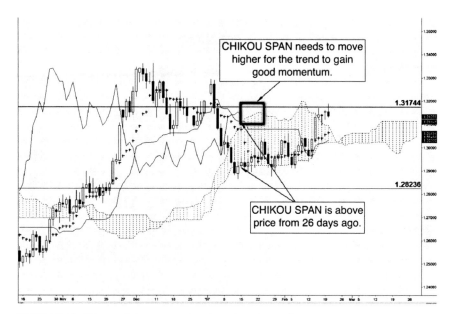

FIGURE 3.19 TradeStation Daily Ichimoku Chart of EURUSD Feb 20, 2007

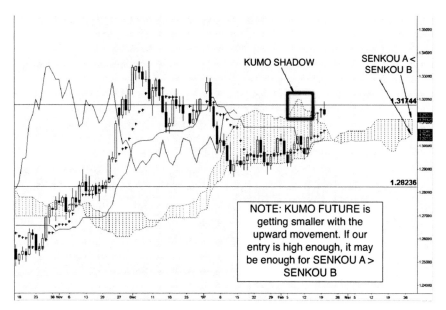

FIGURE 3.20 TradeStation Daily Ichimoku Chart of EURUSD Feb 19, 2007

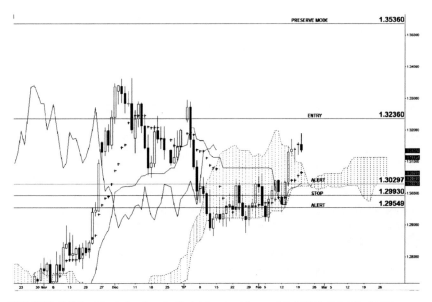

FIGURE 3.21   TradeStation Daily Ichimoku Chart of EURUSD Feb 20, 2007

Action: Set up a bullish entry and bearish alert according to the trading plan. Figure 3.21 illustrates the charts with the entry, stop, alerts, and so forth.

- Entry: Major Resistance = 1.3196, Entry = Major Resistance + Entry Buffer (40) = 1.3236.
- Stop: Kijun Sen = 1.3033: Stop = Kijun Sen minus Exit Buffer (40) = 1.2993.
- Preserve Mode: Change Stop to Tenkan Sen = Entry + 300 pips = 1.3486.

Please note: There is an alert set up at the Kijun Sen as well. If the bullish entry is not triggered and price crosses the Kijun Sen then the alert will tell us to remove the entry and place a bullish alert instead.

Figure 3.22 shows the chart for the EURUSD a couple days later on February 27, 2007. On the day of entry, you have to:

- Verify all Ichimoku indicators are "ok." If anything is not, exit the position right away.
- Verify price has not "escaped" Tenkan Sen or Kijun Sen. If so, follow trading plan and exit if needed.
- Adjust Stops and Alerts. After adjusting your stops and alerts, if the risk is now greater than the one allocated in the trading plan, exit right away.

FIGURE 3.22 TradeStation Daily Ichimoku Chart of EURUSD Feb 27, 2007

The trade was entered on February 27, 2007 (Figure 3.22). Table 3.1 shows the entry trade statistics.

Now, we need to follow the money management section of our trading plan *step by step* without any exceptions. Money management is where it will make the difference on whether you will be a successful trader. Follow your trading plan!

Figure 3.23 shows the trade on March 9, 2007. We have adjusted our stop according to our trading plan. Once that has been done, we continue with the backtest.

Figure 3.24 shows the trade on April 12, 2007. The trend has been developing nicely. In fact, we now have a "Free Trade." A "Free Trade" is where the stop is above the entry for a bullish position. Basically, if we get

TABLE 3.1 Entry Trade Statistics for EURUSD for Feb 27, 2007, Trade #1

Statistics	Value
Entry Date	Feb 27, 2007
Entry Price	1.3236
Entry Stop	1.3026
Entry Risk	210 pips

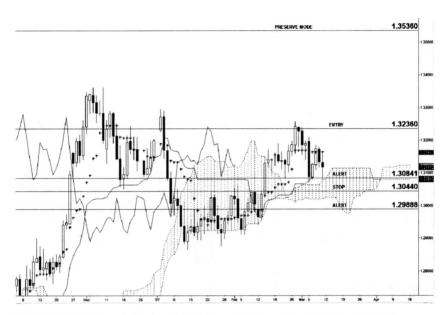

FIGURE 3.23   TradeStation Daily Ichimoku Chart of EURUSD Mar 9, 2007

FIGURE 3.24   TradeStation Daily Ichimoku Chart of EURUSD Apr 12, 2007

FIGURE 3.25 TradeStation Daily Ichimoku Chart of EURUSD Apr 19, 2007

stopped out today, we will not lose anything. In many trading plans, this is where another position can be added because the risk for the first position has been removed.

On April 19, 2007, we entered Preserve mode as illustrated in Figure 3.25. Preserve mode is where we move our stop from the Kijun Sen to the Tenkan Sen to tighten our current stop. We do not want to give back all our profits. There is a saying in the market "it is easy to make money but hard to keep it." When people start to make money they typically start to get greedy. This is the trade that is going to make them a millionaire. As a result, these traders violate their trading plan and stay in the trade when they should exit. With this conservative strategy, we are going to get stopped out for a profit or get stopped out for a minimum loss when we are wrong. With the current stop, we are guaranteed 200 pips if we get stopped out the following day. Notice: We are adjusting our bearish alert as per our trading plan. Do not forget about adjusting the bearish alert even though you are in a bullish trade. Price can drastically change tomorrow.

Figure 3.26 shows the trade on the exit day of May 2, 2007. For every trade, you need to record all the statistics so post-analysis can be performed to track your performance for the trading plan and also to determine if you need to optimize your strategy at the end of the month. Table 3.2 shows the exit trade statistics for May 2, 2007.

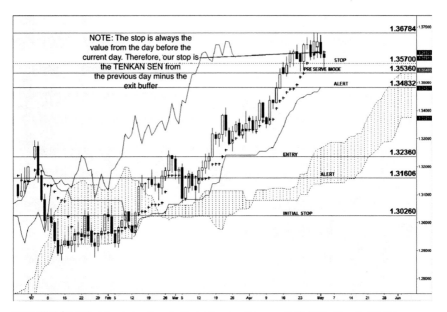

FIGURE 3.26   TradeStation Daily Ichimoku Chart of EURUSD May 2, 2007

TABLE 3.2   Trade Statistics for EURUSD for Trade #1

Statistics	Value
Entry Date	Feb 27, 2007
Entry Price	1.3236
Entry Stop	1.3026
Entry Risk	210 pips
Exit Date	May 2, 2007
Exit Price	1.3570
Profit	334
Max Profit	445 (1.3681 − 1.3236)
Max Drawdown	1.3236 − 1.3072 = 164
Risk/Reward	0.63
Comment	We took more than 50% of the max profit, which is good. This strategy is designed to take around 40% of the max profit because it is a high-probability strategy. Also, notice the duration of this trade. It was a nice trend. It took a long time, so there is a high probability of a trend continuation trade to come.

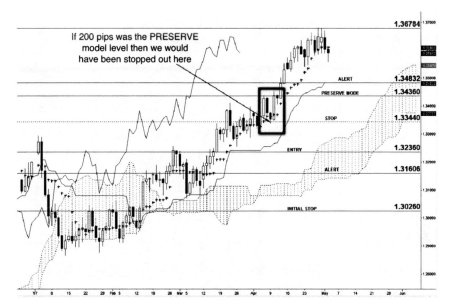

FIGURE 3.27 TradeStation Daily Ichimoku Chart of EURUSD May 2, 2007

Before we continue with the backtest, let us look at the scenario where our trading plan had 200 pips instead of 300 pips for Preserve mode. What would happen? You can see the results in Figure 3.27. The charts show that we would have been stopped out of the trade at the early part of the trend.

Since our trade exited, we need to set up for a new trade. Figure 3.28 shows the new chart setup. Here are the things to note on the chart:

- Price from the Kijun Sen is less than 300 pips so we did not violate our trading plan. If the price was around 312 that is still okay because, if you recall, your entry is higher than where it is now. You are assuming all the Ichimoku values will adjust with the move higher and come within range because they were not off too much to begin with. In the worst-case scenario, if you enter a trade and the values are out of "boundary" then exit the trade right away.
- Chikou Span is still in "Open Space."
- No major pullback has occurred yet. Therefore, this is still part of the major trend.

In examining the chart, you can notice that we have set up for a trend continuation trade because all the Ichimoku indicators are still good. Since the trend has started, a major pullback has not occurred. Price has yet to

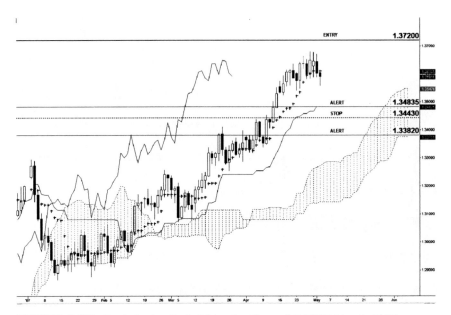

FIGURE 3.28 TradeStation Daily Ichimoku Chart of EURUSD May 2, 2007

penetrate the Kijun Sen to register a major pullback. Therefore, we need to be careful in entering continuation trades before a major pullback has occurred. Our current trading plan mentions nothing about entering continuation trades without a major pullback once a trend has been established. We will now move forward with our backtest.

On May 10, 2007, our Kijun Sen alert got triggered as shown in Figure 3.29. Our trading plan dictates that we change the entry to an alert. We had chosen to do this in the trading plan because when price crosses over the Kijun Sen, it indicates a trend change. With a possible trend change, we do not want to keep a "floating entry." Figure 3.30 shows the new chart setup.

On June 8, 2007, our bearish alert was triggered (Figure 3.31). In the Ichimoku analysis, we have two concerns. The first concern is that both the TS and KS are in the Kumo Cloud and the second concern is that the next support is at 1.3291, which is less than 50 pips away. In order to resolve both of these items, we are going to place an entry below the *next* support level (Figure 3.32). When price enters at that value both the issues should be resolved. If not, we will exit on the day we entered. Notice how we are predicting where we want price to be in order to resolve all the Ichimoku conflicts? You have to be able to do that in order to trade Ichimoku.

On June 22, 2007, our Kijun Sen Alert was triggered (Figure 3.33). Therefore, our entries now become alerts. Notice how close we were to entering the bearish trade (Figure 3.34)? We missed it by 5 pips! If we

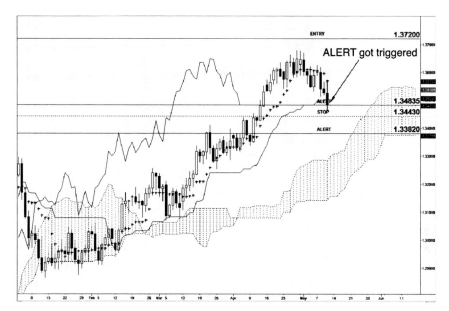

FIGURE 3.29 TradeStation Daily Ichimoku Chart of EURUSD May 10, 2007

FIGURE 3.30 TradeStation Daily Ichimoku Chart of EURUSD May 10, 2007

FIGURE 3.31 TradeStation Daily Ichimoku Chart of EURUSD June 8, 2007

FIGURE 3.32 TradeStation Daily Ichimoku Chart of EURUSD June 8, 2007

FIGURE 3.33 TradeStation Daily Ichimoku Chart of EURUSD June 22, 2007

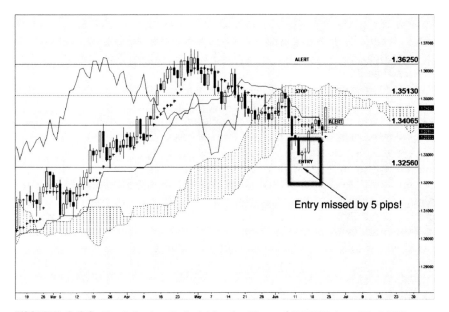

FIGURE 3.34 TradeStation Daily Ichimoku Chart of EURUSD June 22, 2007

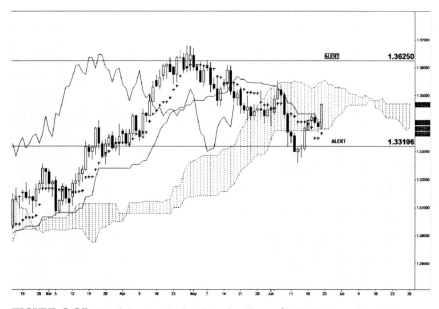

FIGURE 3.35 TradeStation Daily Ichimoku Chart of EURUSD June 22, 2007

entered the trade, we would have taken a loss. The buffer kept us out
of this trade. Backtesting with different buffers is something that everyone needs to do to find the optimized buffer value. This is part of the
optimized section.

Figure 3.35 shows the new chart setup after the entry values were removed. The chart displays the bullish and the bearish alerts. Notice that
we placed the bullish alert very high. We did not even attempt to put an
entry above the top of the Kumo Cloud because there are not more than
50 pips between resistance values. The safest thing to do was to place an
alert below the ultimate high indicated on the chart.

On July 2, 2007, our bullish alert was triggered (Figure 3.36). In our
Ichimoku analysis, we have two concerns. The first is that the Tenkan Sen
and the Kijun Sen are in the Kumo Cloud. With an entry at 1.3715, which
is 35 pips above the previous high, the TS and KS should exit the Kumo
Cloud with no problems because it is thin. The second is if we set up a
stop of KS – 35-pip buffer, the stop would be 1.3414 and our entry would be
1.3715. This is a distance of 301, which is more than 300 pips according to
our trading plan. Because this is not a significant difference, we are going
to move forward with the entry assuming that an entry price would have
equalized within 300 pips from the KS. If not, we will use TS as our stop
according to our trading plan at entry (Figure 3.37).

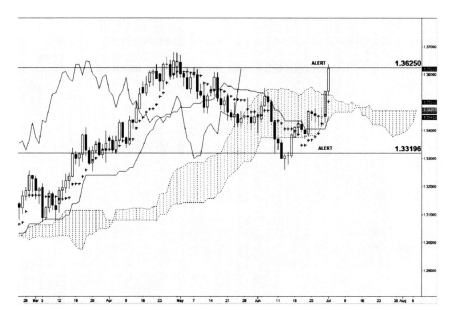

FIGURE 3.36 TradeStation Daily Ichimoku Chart of EURUSD July 2, 2007

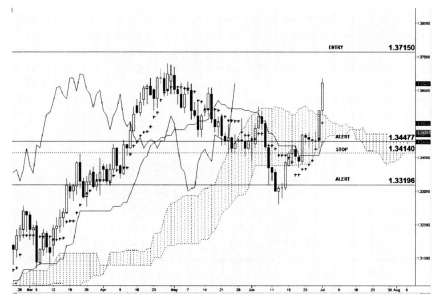

FIGURE 3.37 TradeStation Daily Ichimoku Chart of EURUSD July 2, 2007

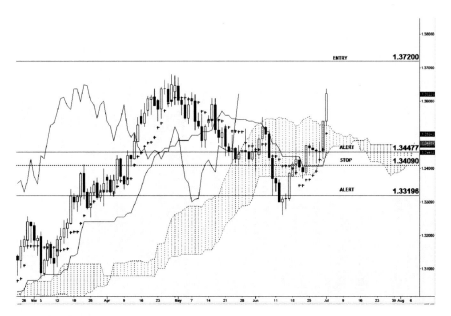

FIGURE 3.38 TradeStation Daily Ichimoku Chart of EURUSD July 2, 2007

Are we ready to move forward now? If you said "yes" then you just violated your trading plan. Do you see where we violated the trading plan?

If you found the mistake we made, *congratulations*! If you did not find the mistake then you need to revisit your trading plan and study it further. This is your guide to being successful. The mistake is that we used the short side (bearish) buffer for entry and also for the stop. We are supposed to use 40 pips instead of 35. Figure 3.38 illustrates the correct values for the entry and the stop.

On July 10, 2007, our trade entered on the bullish side (Figure 3.39). Table 3.3 shows all the trade entry statistics.

On July 31, 2007, we were almost stopped out (Figure 3.40). Notice how the 40-pip buffer is working well. We missed the stop by 5 pips! In Chapter 4, we talk about optimizing the trading plan. During this discussion, we talk about changing our buffer. In order to optimize your trading plan to maximum profits and minimize losses, you have to take note of small things such as missing the stop by 5 pips as you are backtesting. This way, you have some idea of what you can try during the optimization stage. Throughout the book, I provide "hints" on different things you can try during the optimization phrase.

On August 9, 2007, we were stopped out of the trade with a loss (Figure 3.41). Table 3.4 illustrates the trade statistics for Trade #2.

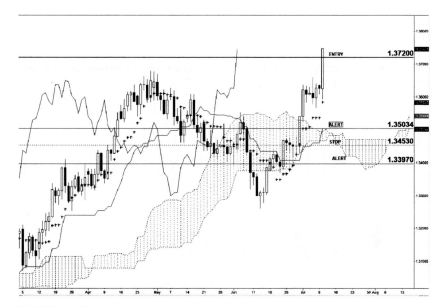

FIGURE 3.39 TradeStation Daily Ichimoku Chart of EURUSD July 10, 2007

FIGURE 3.40 TradeStation Daily Ichimoku Chart of EURUSD July 31, 2007

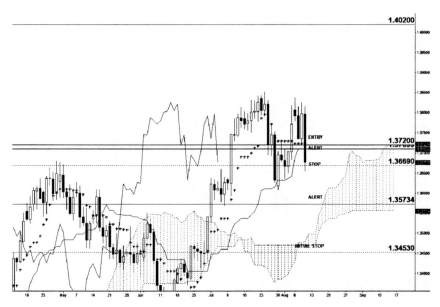

FIGURE 3.41 TradeStation Daily Ichimoku Chart of EURUSD Aug 9, 2007

Notice that we lost 46 pips compared to our initial risk stop of 267 pips. Rarely will you get stopped out at the initial risk. There are only two chances of this occurring:

1. Ichimoku charts were not interpreted correctly. Someone did not look at all five Ichimoku indicators and make sure that *all* were good.
2. Random events in the market where the instrument gapped drastically in a short period of time. This can happen and this is why we *always* use a stop and never risk 100 percent of our portfolio at one time (money management).

TABLE 3.3 Entry Trade Statistics for EURUSD for July 10, 2007, Trade #2

Statistics	Value
Entry Date	July 10, 2007
Entry Price	1.3720
Entry Stop	1.3453
Entry Risk	267 pips

TABLE 3.4 Trade Statistics for EURUSD for Trade #2

Statistics	Value
Entry Date	July 10, 2007
Entry Price	1.3720
Entry Stop	1.3453
Entry Risk	267 pips
Exit Date	August 9, 2007
Exit Price	1.3669
Profit	$1.3669 - 1.3720 = -51$ (loss)
Max Profit	$1.3851 - 1.3720 = 131$ pips
Max Drawdown	$1.3720 - 1.3608 = 112$ pips
Risk/Reward	N/A
Comment	We were wrong . . .

Figure 3.42 shows the chart setup with the alerts. Can you guess why we did not set up an entry for a bullish continuation trade again?

The reason is that the Chikou Span is close to price. Therefore, it is dangerous to place an entry again. There is no harm in placing an alert because it will trigger before a possible entry.

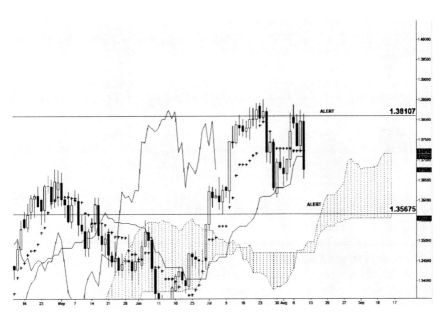

FIGURE 3.42 TradeStation Daily Ichimoku Chart of EURUSD Aug 9, 2007

FIGURE 3.43 TradeStation Daily Ichimoku Chart of EURUSD Aug 14, 2007

On August 14, 2007, the bearish alert was triggered (Figure 3.43). In examining the charts, the Ichimoku indicators illustrate that we are *not* ready for an entry yet (Figure 3.44). Therefore, we are going to reset our alerts again and continue with the backtest (Figure 3.45).

On Aug 15, 2007, the bearish alert triggered again (Figure 3.46). Again, the charts are not ready for an entry signal yet. Figure 3.47 illustrates the reason why we will not place an entry. A pullback will probably set up a bearish trade equalizing all the Ichimoku variables.

Figure 3.48 shows the chart with the new alerts. Both alerts are set up to trigger right before the Kumo shadow top/bottom. We have done this in order to set up entries for breaking out of the Kumo shadow.

Figure 3.49 shows that the bearish alert has been triggered. In the last three days, we have had three big movements that have been pushing our alerts down more and more. We have *not* entered a trade due to the Ichimoku signals not being set up yet. Yes, we did miss the big move but remember we have not lost any money. Maybe one of the other currency pairs you are trading did not have price extended like the EURUSD did at this time. One of the goals for our trading plan is for it to work for all time frames and all currency instruments. Of course, there will be some exceptions but in general it should work for the majority of instruments.

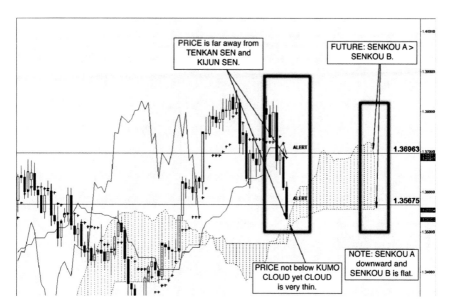

FIGURE 3.44 TradeStation Daily Ichimoku Chart of EURUSD Aug 14, 2007

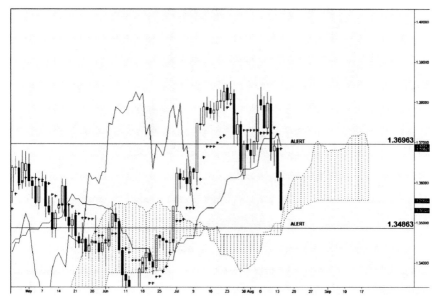

FIGURE 3.45 TradeStation Daily Ichimoku Chart of EURUSD Aug 14, 2007

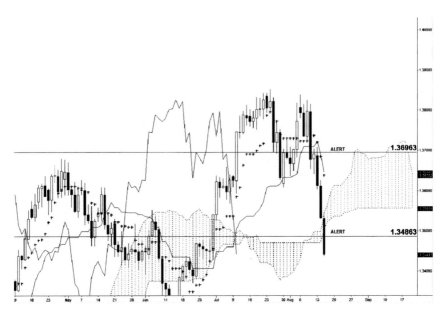

FIGURE 3.46 TradeStation Daily Ichimoku Chart of EURUSD Aug 15, 2007

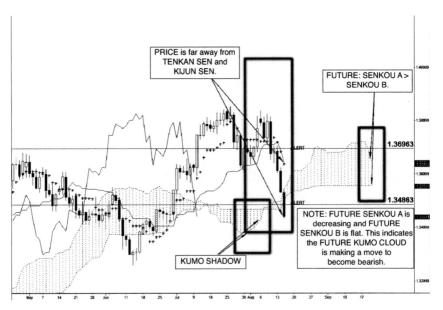

FIGURE 3.47 TradeStation Daily Ichimoku Chart of EURUSD Aug 15, 2007

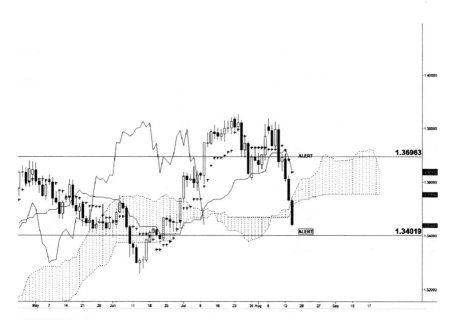

FIGURE 3.48 TradeStation Daily Ichimoku Chart of EURUSD Aug 15, 2007

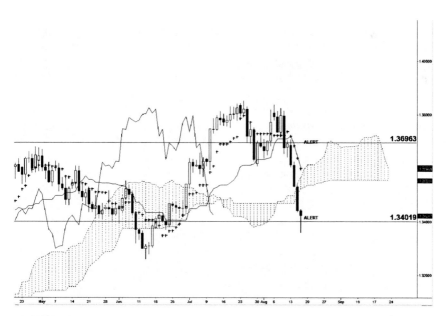

FIGURE 3.49 TradeStation Daily Ichimoku Chart of EURUSD Aug 16, 2007

FIGURE 3.50 TradeStation Daily Ichimoku Chart of EURUSD Aug 16, 2007

The goal is to keep it "simple." We are not going to adjust our trading plan at this time just to capture this movement. If you do, you are "curve fitting," which is not a good idea. The people that "curve fit" will never have a stable trading plan because it is like a revolving door, changing over and over.

So, are the charts ready for an entry now? Is Figure 3.50 correct? If you said "Yes" then you violated your trading plan. Remember, we are trading the short side (i.e., Bearish). The Bearish side has a different set of rules then the bullish. Figure 3.51 displays the charts with the correct bearish values according to our trading plan.

Notice in Figure 3.51 that the distance of price from Tenkan Sen and Kijun Sen was outside the range according to our trading plan. As a result, we cannot place an entry; instead we have to use an alert for now (Figure 3.52).

On August 31, 2007, the Bullish alert was triggered as illustrated in Figure 3.53. After a couple of bearish alerts being triggered, price reversed and went bullish. Figure 3.54 shows the Ichimoku analysis of the chart.

Overall, if we choose a nice bullish entry, all the Ichimoku indicators should be supporting a bullish trade. Therefore, we are going to set up

FIGURE 3.51 TradeStation Daily Ichimoku Chart of EURUSD Aug 16, 2007

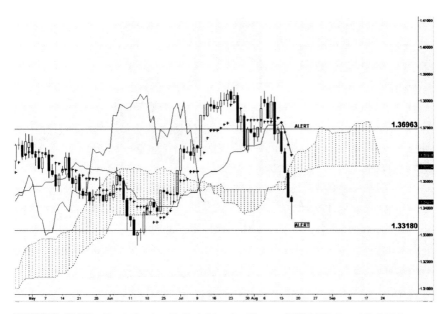

FIGURE 3.52 TradeStation Daily Ichimoku Chart of EURUSD Aug 16, 2007

FIGURE 3.53 TradeStation Daily Ichimoku Chart of EURUSD Aug 31, 2007

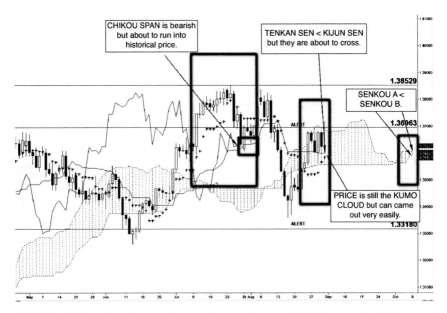

FIGURE 3.54 TradeStation Daily Ichimoku Chart of EURUSD Aug 31, 2007

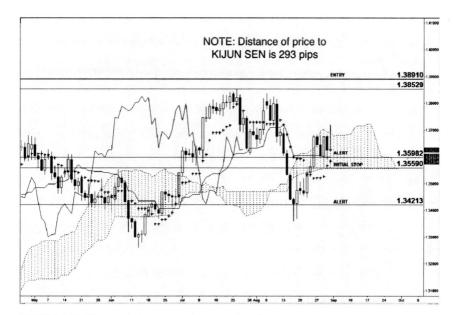

FIGURE 3.55 TradeStation Daily Ichimoku Chart of EURUSD Aug 31, 2007

for a bullish entry. Figure 3.55 illustrates the chart with the entry, stops, and alerts. We choose the entry above the high established in July because every entry before that value would violate our trading plan of making sure there were 50 pips to the next resistance. With this entry, we are still within the 300 pips of price to the Kijun Sen.

On September 12, 2007, a trade was entered on the bullish side (see Figure 3.56 for details). The entry statistics are shown in Table 3.5.

Figure 3.57 shows the chart one week after entry. We are adjusting our stop and alerts every day. Also, we have to monitor price versus Tenkan Sen to make sure they are within limits at all times. Basically, we are following our trading plan. I know I have repeated many things over and over but it is *needed*. The goal is to learn through repetition.

Figure 3.58 illustrates the chart for EURUSD on September 28, 2007. (The trade statistics are shown in Table 3.6.) On this day, our trade went into Preserve mode. Also, we now have a free trade, which means we will make a profit even if we get stopped out now. Notice that the closing price is 1.4267 and the value of the Tenkan Sen is 1.4053, which is a 214-pip difference. Our trading plan had stated that if price was 200 pips away from Tenkan Sen, we should exit. As a result, we should exit, right? Yes, because that is in our trading plan. Figure 3.59 shows the chart with the exit statistics.

FIGURE 3.56 TradeStation Daily Ichimoku Chart of EURUSD Sept 12, 2007

If you reached this point and have *not* noticed a mistake then you are not paying attention to your trading plan at all. I am purposely putting errors all over the place to make sure you follow your trading plan. If you do not follow your trading plan then you are gambling instead of being a system trader.

In our trading plan, it mentions that you exit when price is 200 pips or more away from the Tenkan Sen *when it is flat*. If you look at the charts, the Tenkan is not flat so we should not exit. When a trend is occurring as the Tenkan Sen is indicating by pointing upward, you want to "ride" the trend as far as you can take it. There will be many situations where price has escaped the Tenkan Sen and keeps on going. Those

TABLE 3.5 Entry Trade Statistics for EURUSD on Sept 12, 2007, Trade #3

Statistics	Value
Entry Date	Sept 12, 2007
Entry Price	1.3891
Entry Stop	1.3594
Entry Risk	297 pips

FIGURE 3.57 TradeStation Daily Ichimoku Chart of EURUSD Sept 19, 2007

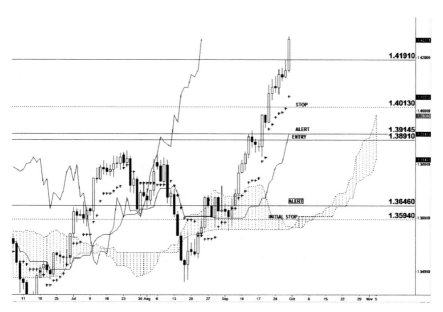

FIGURE 3.58 TradeStation Daily Ichimoku Chart of EURUSD Sept 28, 2007

TABLE 3.6 Trade Statistics for EURUSD on Sept 28, 2007, Trade #3

Statistics	Value
Entry Date	Sept 12, 2007
Entry Price	1.3891
Entry Stop	1.3594
Entry Risk	297 pips
Exit Date	Sept 28, 2007
Exit Price	1.4267
Profit	$1.4267 - 1.3891 = 376$ pips
Max Profit	387 pips
Max Drawdown	64 pips
Risk/Reward	$297/376 = 0.80$
Comment	

situations occur mainly when the Tenkan Sen is pointing in the direction of the trend instead of being flat. Let us now go back and correct the mistake. We will continue with the trade because we should never have exited the trade at all.

On October 3, 2007, the trade exited with a profit as shown in Figure 3.60. Table 3.7 shows the actual trade statistics for Trade #3.

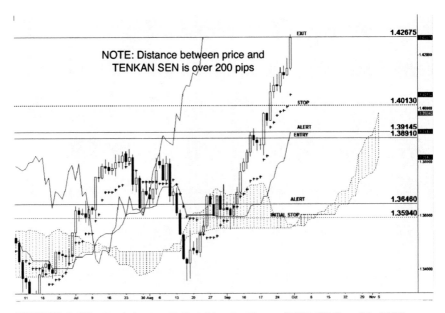

FIGURE 3.59 TradeStation Daily Ichimoku Chart of EURUSD Sept 28, 2007

FIGURE 3.60 TradeStation Daily Ichimoku Chart of EURUSD Oct 3, 2007

TABLE 3.7 Trade Statistics for EURUSD on Oct 3, 2007, actual Trade #3

Statistics	Value
Entry Date	Sept 12, 2007
Entry Price	1.3891
Entry Stop	1.3594
Entry Risk	297 pips
Entry Date	Oct 3, 2007
Exit Price	1.4120
Profit	1.4120 − 1.3891 = 229 pips
Max Profit	1.4280 − 1.3891 = 389 pips
Max Drawdown	1.3891 − 1.3827 = 64 pips
Risk/Reward	297/229 = 1.30
Comment	It turns out that if we exited when price was far away from the Tenkan Sen, we would have taken the Max profit for this trade. This could be an optimization technique that can be tested. Basically, you get out when price is far from the Tenkan Sen and then place another entry above the last high just in case the trend decides to continue.

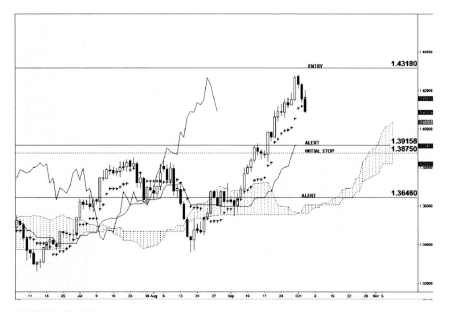

FIGURE 3.61 TradeStation Daily Ichimoku Chart of EURUSD Oct 3, 2007

We now continue with the testing because we have closed out our bullish trade. Figure 3.61 illustrates the alert and the new entry. Since the Chikou Span is still in an "open space," we are going to be looking for a trend continuation trade. Note that there has not been a major pullback as of yet.

October 19, 2007, a bullish trade was entered as illustrated in Figure 3.62. The entry statistics are listed in Table 3.8.

Figure 3.63 shows the chart on November 2, 2007. We are getting close to Preserve mode but are not there yet. Our risk has now been reduced to less than 100 pips.

Figure 3.64 illustrates the chart for November 7, 2007. On this date, we now have entered Preserve mode so our risk has been minimized completely. In fact, we are now in a "free trade," too. We are guaranteed to make 150-plus pips.

November 12, 2007, the bullish trade exited with a profit as illustrated in Figure 3.65. The trade statistics are listed in Table 3.9.

Figure 3.66 illustrates the new alerts and the new entry price. The Chikou Span is in "open space" so we are going to look for trend continuation trade. Note that no major pullbacks have occurred yet.

FIGURE 3.62 TradeStation Daily Ichimoku Chart of EURUSD Oct 19, 2007

TABLE 3.8 Entry Trade Statistics for EURUSD on Oct 19, 2007, Trade #4

Statistics	Value
Entry Date	Oct 19, 2007
Entry Price	1.4318
Entry Stop	1.4042
Entry Risk	276 pips

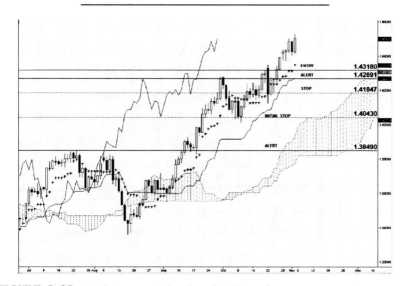

FIGURE 3.63 TradeStation Daily Ichimoku Chart of EURUSD Nov 2, 2007

FIGURE 3.64   TradeStation Daily Ichimoku Chart of EURUSD Nov 7, 2007

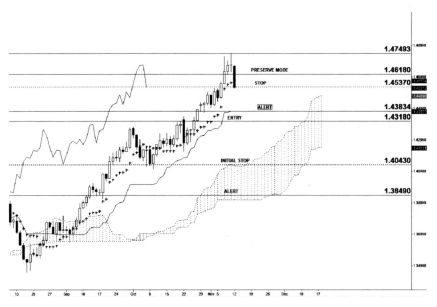

FIGURE 3.65   TradeStation Daily Ichimoku Chart of EURUSD Nov 12, 2007

TABLE 3.9 Trade Statistics for EURUSD on Nov 12, 2007, Trade #4

Statistics	Value
Entry Date	Oct 19, 2007
Entry Price	1.4318
Entry Stop	1.4042
Entry Risk	276 pips
Exit Date	Nov 12, 2007
Exit Price	1.45370
Profit	1.4537 − 1.4318 = 219 pips
Max Profit	1.4749 − 1.4318 = 431 pips
Max Drawdown	1.43180 − 1.4169 = 149
Risk/Reward	276/219 = 1.26
Comment	We capture 50% of the max profit

On November 20, 2007, a bullish trade was entered as shown in Figure 3.67. The entry trade statistics are shown in Table 3.10.

The distance between price and Kijun Sen is 306, without the entry buffer. This is above the 300-pip distance that we are willing to accept. Should we override the trading plan because it is only 6 pips? If you override it now, you may make this a habit and if that happens, why have a trading plan? We do not want to override so we will exit the trade right away. The exit statistics are listed in Table 3.11.

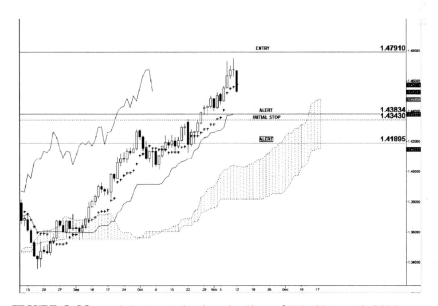

FIGURE 3.66 TradeStation Daily Ichimoku Chart of EURUSD Nov 12, 2007

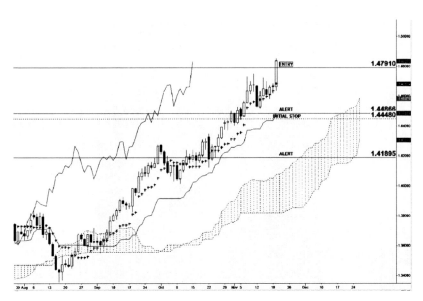

FIGURE 3.67 TradeStation Daily Ichimoku Chart of EURUSD Nov 20, 2007

TABLE 3.10 Entry Trade Statistics for EURUSD on Nov 20, 2007, Trade #5

Statistics	Value
Entry Date	Nov 20, 2007
Entry Price	1.4791
Entry Stop	1.4448
Entry Risk	343 pips

TABLE 3.11 Trade Statistics for EURUSD on Nov 20, 2007, Trade #5

Statistics	Value
Entry Date	Nov 20, 2007
Entry Price	1.4791
Entry Stop	1.4448
Entry Risk	343 pips
Exit Date	Nov 20, 2007
Exit Price	1.4838
Profit	47
Max Profit	61
Max Drawdown	N/A
Comment	Trade was exited because of price distance to Tenkan Sen

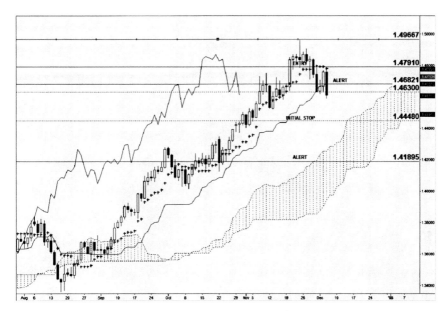

FIGURE 3.68 TradeStation Daily Ichimoku Chart of EURUSD Dec 5, 2007

Let us examine what would have happened if we continued with the trade. Figure 3.68 illustrates the exit of the trade on December 5, 2007, with a loss. The statistics for the trade as listed in Table 3.12.

Figure 3.69 illustrates the new alerts on December 5, 2007. We did not enter a trend continuation trade because the Chikou Span is too close to historical price.

The charts in Figure 3.70 show that the bearish alert has been triggered. There is really no trade because price is now below the Kumo Cloud.

TABLE 3.12 Trade Statistics for EURUSD on Dec 5, 2007, Trade #5 simulation

Statistics	Value
Entry Date	Nov 20, 2007
Entry Price	1.4791
Entry Stop	1.4448
Entry Risk	343 pips
Exit Date	Dec 5, 2007
Exit Price	1.4630
Profit	−161 (Loss)
Comment	Simulated trade ...

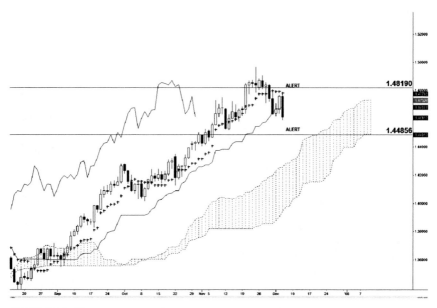

FIGURE 3.69   TradeStation Daily Ichimoku Chart of EURUSD Dec 5, 2007

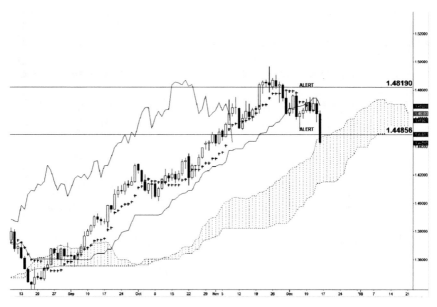

FIGURE 3.70   TradeStation Daily Ichimoku Chart of EURUSD Dec 14, 2007

FIGURE 3.71 TradeStation Daily Ichimoku Chart of EURUSD Dec 14, 2007

Figure 3.71 illustrates the new alerts. We continue moving forward with our backtesting almost completing one year.

The bearish alert in Figure 3.72 was triggered on December 20, 2007. Price is still not below the Kumo Cloud so we are going to reset the alerts (Figure 3.73).

In Figure 3.74, the bullish alert was triggered. We are still not ready for a bullish entry according to Figure 3.75.

Figure 3.76 shows the charts with the new bearish and bullish alerts. We chose the bullish alert much higher this time because we need a big upward movement to cause the Tenkan Sen and the Kijun Sen to cross along with moving the Chikou Span away from the historical price.

On January 4, 2008, the bullish alert was triggered (Figure 3.77). Figure 3.78 shows that the Ichimoku indicators are still not ready for a bullish entry. Therefore, we have reset the alerts, which are shown in Figure 3.79.

Figure 3.80 illustrates that the bullish alert was triggered on January 14, 2008. In examining the Ichimoku chart for that date, all the indicators are "prime" for an entry. The entry information is shown in Figure 3.81. From the chart, it is apparent that we still cannot enter. This time, the issue is price from the Kijun Sen. Therefore, we have reset the alerts and wait again as illustrated in Figure 3.82.

FIGURE 3.72 TradeStation Daily Ichimoku Chart of EURUSD Dec 20, 2007

FIGURE 3.73 TradeStation Daily Ichimoku Chart of EURUSD Dec 20, 2007

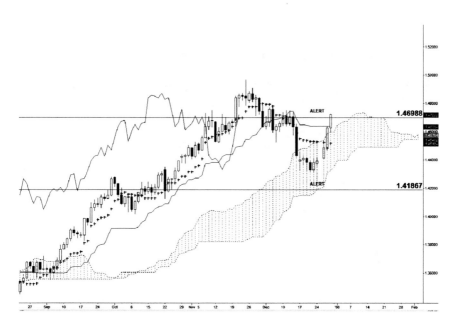

FIGURE 3.74 TradeStation Daily Ichimoku Chart of EURUSD Dec 28, 2007

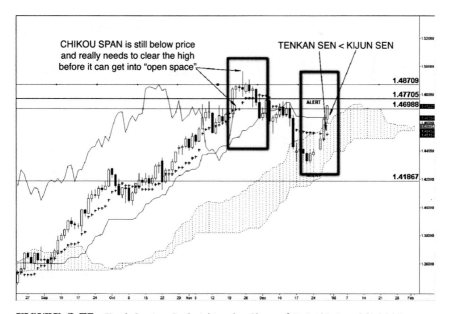

FIGURE 3.75 TradeStation Daily Ichimoku Chart of EURUSD Dec 28, 2007

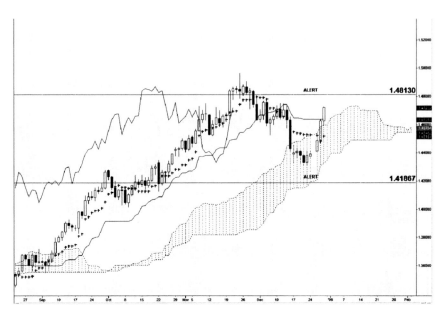

FIGURE 3.76   TradeStation Daily Ichimoku Chart of EURUSD Dec 28, 2007

FIGURE 3.77   TradeStation Daily Ichimoku Chart of EURUSD Jan 4, 2008

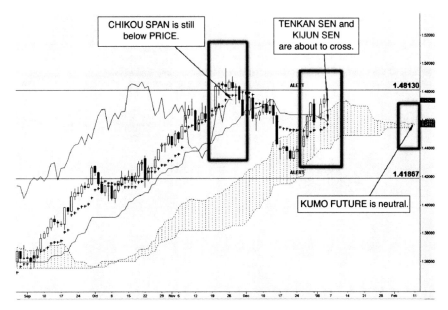

FIGURE 3.78 TradeStation Daily Ichimoku Chart of EURUSD Jan 4, 2008

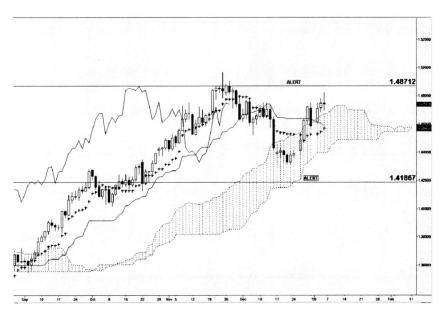

FIGURE 3.79 TradeStation Daily Ichimoku Chart of EURUSD Jan 4, 2008

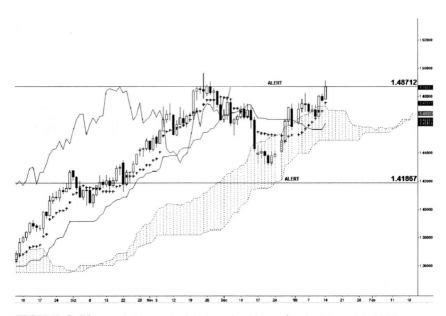

FIGURE 3.80 TradeStation Daily Ichimoku Chart of EURUSD Jan 14, 2008

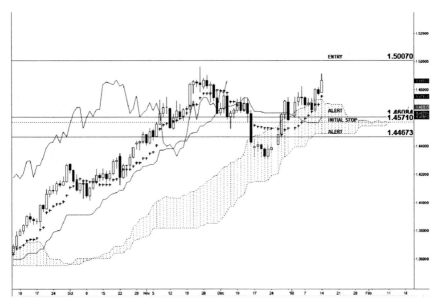

FIGURE 3.81 TradeStation Daily Ichimoku Chart of EURUSD Jan 14, 2008

FIGURE 3.82 TradeStation Daily Ichimoku Chart of EURUSD Jan 14, 2008

On January 21, 2008, the bearish alert was triggered (Figure 3.83). At this time, the Ichimoku indicators are not ready for a bearish entry at all as illustrated in Figure 3.84. Figure 3.85 shows the new alerts since we cannot enter a trade.

On February 1, 2008, the bullish alert was triggered as illustrated in Figure 3.86. The Ichimoku indicators would be fine if we selected a bullish entry. However, the problem is that the Tenkan Sen is far from price. It is outside the 200-pip range we have specified in our trading plan. Therefore, we cannot enter at this time. Now, we have to select the new bullish alert. If we go higher than the value we have at this time, we could miss the break. Therefore, we are going to keep the same alert that we had before.

On February 26, 2008, the bullish alert got triggered as shown in Figure 3.87. If you look back to the last possible entry, which we did not enter because of the price being far away from the Tenkan, you will see that it saved us from a loss. This is the reason why we have that in our trading plan. Looking at the charts on February 26, 2008, you see that the Tenkan Sen and price have equalized and we are ready for a trend to begin. All the Ichimoku indicators are set up and ready for the trend. Therefore, we are going to place our entry, alerts, and stops. Figure 3.88 illustrates this information.

FIGURE 3.83 TradeStation Daily Ichimoku Chart of EURUSD Jan 21, 2008

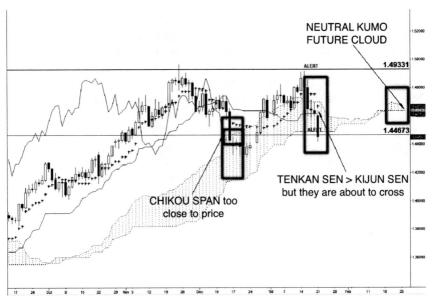

FIGURE 3.84 TradeStation Daily Ichimoku Chart of EURUSD Jan 21, 2008

FIGURE 3.85 TradeStation Daily Ichimoku Chart of EURUSD Jan 21, 2008

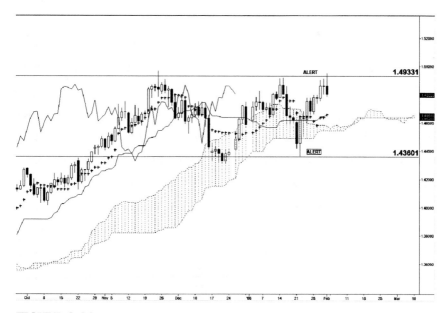

FIGURE 3.86 TradeStation Daily Ichimoku Chart of EURUSD Feb 1, 2008

FIGURE 3.87 TradeStation Daily Ichimoku Chart of EURUSD Feb 26, 2008

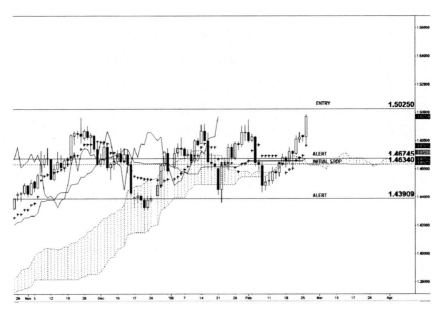

FIGURE 3.88 TradeStation Daily Ichimoku Chart of EURUSD Feb 26, 2008

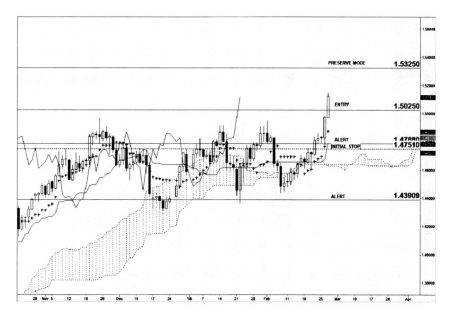

FIGURE 3.89 TradeStation Daily Ichimoku Chart of EURUSD Feb 27, 2008

On February 27, 2008, we entered a bullish trade as shown in Figure 3.89. The entry statistics are shown in Table. 3.13.

Notice that price is at 1.5119 and the Tenkan Sen is at 1.4876. This is more than 200 pips away. Therefore, we have to exit the trade according to our trading plan. The exit statistics are shown in Table 3.14.

Wait a minute, is the Tenkan Sen flat? No, it is not, and that 200-pip rule for Tenkan Sen is when it is *flat*. We hope you caught this mistake. If you did not catch it, you have to do something different now to learn because what you are doing is not working. You are not retaining the trading plan information. One suggestion that I recommend to all of my students is to print and laminate the trading plan, both the bullish and the bearish trading plans. Once laminated, hang it on top or bottom of the computer screen

TABLE 3.13 Entry Trade Statistics for EURUSD on Feb 27, 2008, Trade #6

Statistics	Value
Entry Date	Feb 27, 2008
Entry Price	1.5025
Entry Stop	1.4751
Entry Risk	274 pips

TABLE 3.14   Trade Statistics for EURUSD on Feb 27, 2008, Trade #6

Statistics	Value
Entry Date	Feb 27, 2008
Entry Price	1.5025
Entry Stop	1.4751
Entry Risk	274 pips
Exit Date	Feb 27, 2008
Exit Price	1.5119
Profit	94 pips
Max Profit	118 pips
Risk/Reward	7.29
Comment	Risk/Reward is high since we exited the trade on the same day as entry. Therefore, it is "inflated."

that you use to trade. This way, you will continuously see it over and over. Because it was a mistake, we are going to continue with the open trade and not close it out.

On March 6, 2008, we entered Preserve mode for our bullish trade (Figure 3.90) and are now at a free trade. Notice that every time we enter Preserve mode, it is almost the same day as we get to a free day. That

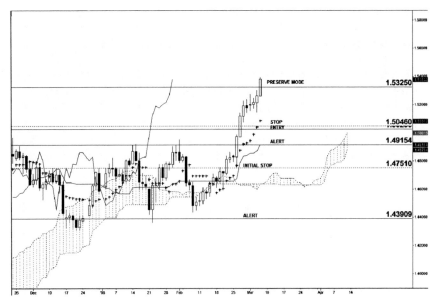

FIGURE 3.90   TradeStation Daily Ichimoku Chart of EURUSD Mar 6, 2008

FIGURE 3.91 TradeStation Daily Ichimoku Chart of EURUSD Mar 20, 2008

has worked out nicely *so far*. It may change later in time but so far it has worked for more than $1^1/_2$ years of backtesting.

On March 20, 2008, we exited our trade with a profit. You can see the chart in Figure 3.91. The trade statistics (Table 3.15) follow.

In this trade, we captured more than 50 percent of the max profit, which is really good. It is hard to capture the entire trend, especially from the beginning of the trend to the end of the trend. With the Ichimoku

TABLE 3.15 Trade Statistics for EURUSD on Mar 20, 2008, Actual Trade #6

Statistics	Value
Entry Date	Feb 27, 2008
Exit Date	Mar 20, 2008
Entry Price	1.5025
Exit Price	1.5553
Profit	528 pip
Entry Risk	274
Max Profit	878
Max Drawdown	N/A
Risk/Reward	0.52

strategy we are using at this time, the goal is to capture 30 percent to 40 percent of the trend. We definitely cannot capture the beginning of the trend because the Chikou looks at 26 periods (i.e., 26 days). Therefore, when the Chikou Span is in "open space," at least 26 days have gone by, which is usually the beginning of the trend. We should not get upset at all about this because it is hard to recognize the beginning of the trend. In addition, there is a lot of "chop chop" at the beginning of a trend because a trend typically proceeds a consolidation period.

We are now going to set up the chart for both Bullish and Bearish alerts. No entry will be placed because the Chikou Span is getting closer to the historical price (Figure 3.92).

On March 26, 2008, our bullish alert was triggered as shown in Figure 3.93. We are now going to set up for a bullish entry because all the Ichimoku indicators are indicating bullish.

Figure 3.94 shows the entry values. Notice how far price is from both Tenkan Sen and Kijun Sen; it is outside our trading plan range. As a result, we cannot enter the trade yet. We have to set up alerts and be patient (Figure 3.95).

On March 31, 2008, the bullish alert was triggered as shown in Figure 3.96. Price is still far away from the Kijun Sen so we will have to reset

FIGURE 3.92 TradeStation Daily Ichimoku Chart of EURUSD Mar 20, 2008

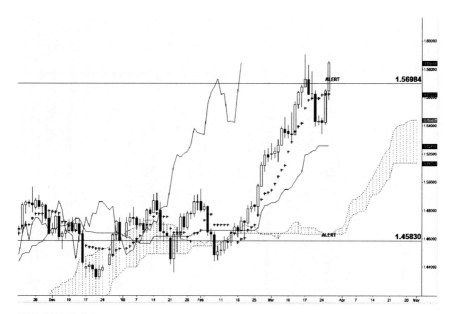

FIGURE 3.93 TradeStation Daily Ichimoku Chart of EURUSD Mar 26, 2008

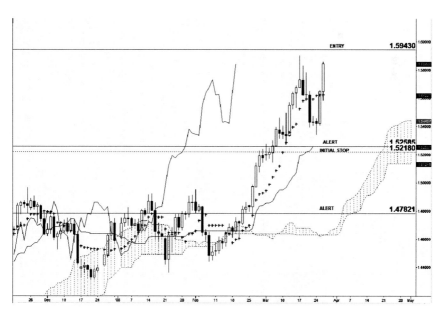

FIGURE 3.94 TradeStation Daily Ichimoku Chart of EURUSD Mar 26, 2008

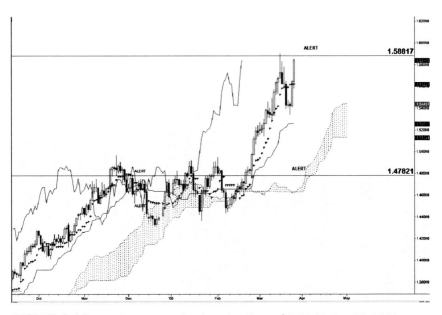

FIGURE 3.95 TradeStation Daily Ichimoku Chart of EURUSD Mar 26, 2008

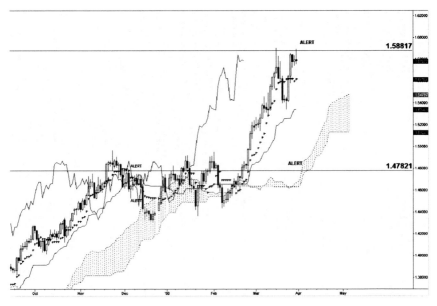

FIGURE 3.96 TradeStation Daily Ichimoku Chart of EURUSD Mar 31, 2008

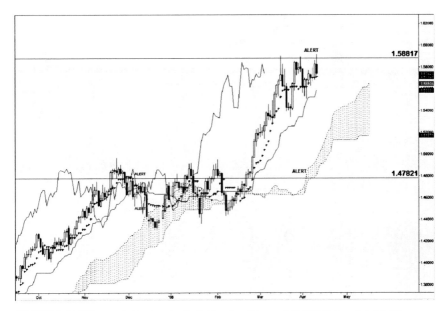

FIGURE 3.97 TradeStation Daily Ichimoku Chart of EURUSD Apr 10, 2008

the alerts and still wait. We are going to keep our alerts in the same place and just move forward with the backtest.

The bullish alert was triggered on April 10, 2008 (Figure 3.97). Price now has equalized with the Kijun Sen so we can set up a bullish entry (Figure 3.98).

On April 16, 2008, a bullish trade was entered and is illustrated in Figure 3.99. This is the second bullish trade we will be entering in the trend. If we did not go into Preserve mode in the previous trade and continued to use the Kijun Sen as a stop, we still would be in the trade at this time. This is an optimization change that *you* can try. The entry trade statistics are shown in Table 3.16.

On April 24, 2008, we were stopped out for a loss for the bullish trade (Figure 3.100). The trade statistics are shown in Table. 3.17.

Wow, this is a 300-plus pip loss. What happened? How can we lose more than 300 pips when we are supposed to have a "safety value" of 300 pips in our trading plan? In our trading plan, we specified price in respect to Tenkan Sen and Kijun Sen without including the buffer. The buffer was 40 pips. That was the reason we exceeded the 300-pip loss value. You should think about this trade and think of different ways on how you can eliminate this loss (i.e., optimization techniques). One change we can make is to say 300-pip loss *including* the buffer. Once you have some ideas, you

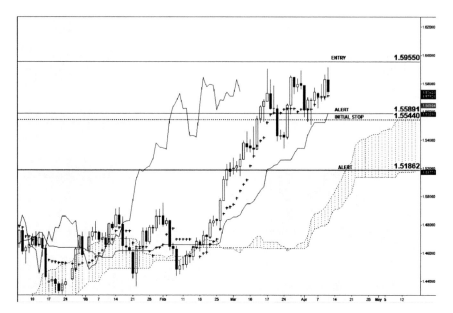

FIGURE 3.98 TradeStation Daily Ichimoku Chart of EURUSD Apr 10, 2008

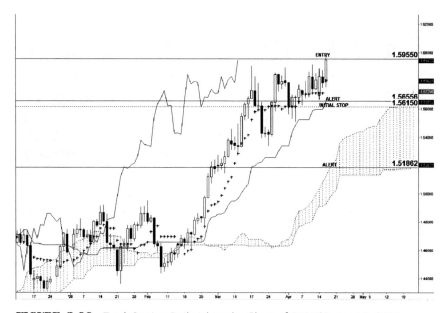

FIGURE 3.99 TradeStation Daily Ichimoku Chart of EURUSD Apr 16, 2008

TABLE 3.16 Entry Trade Statistics for EURUSD on Apr 16, 2008, Trade #7

Statistics	Value
Entry Date	Apr 16, 2008
Entry Price	1.5955
Entry Stop	1.5615
Entry Risk	340 (300 pips from price and Kijun Sen)

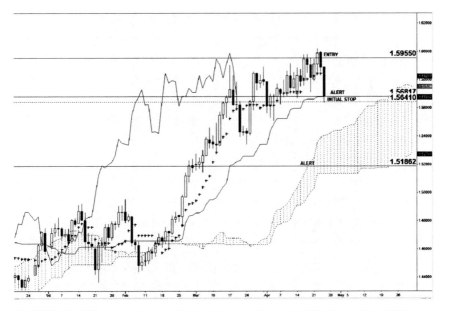

FIGURE 3.100 TradeStation Daily Ichimoku Chart of EURUSD Apr 24, 2008

TABLE 3.17 Trade Statistics for EURUSD on Apr 24, 2008, Trade #7

Statistics	Value
Entry Date	Apr 16, 2008
Entry Price	1.5955
Entry Stop	1.5615
Entry Risk	340 (300 pips from price and Kijun Sen)
Exit Date	Apr 24, 2008
Exit Price	1.5955
Profit	−315
Max Profits	63

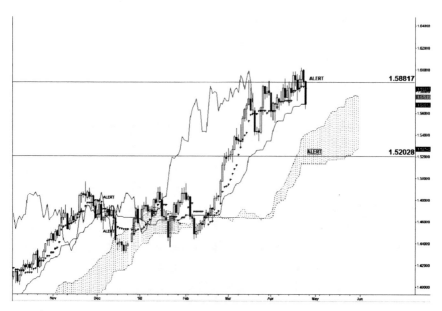

FIGURE 3.101   TradeStation Daily Ichimoku Chart of EURUSD Apr 24, 2008

should alter your trading plan and then backtest again. We discuss this later in the optimization chapter. For now, we will take this loss. Remember, there is *no perfect* system. We *will* have losses; however, the goal is to minimize the losses. This trade was minimized to a 300-pip loss. Figure 3.101 illustrates the alerts that now have been set up. We do not want to enter another bullish position until we get some type of pullback now. We failed at one continuation trend trade without a pullback, but we do not want to fail on two before a pullback has occurred.

More than one month has gone already and none of our alerts have triggered. You can see the chart pattern in Figure 3.102.

On July 2, 2008, our bullish alert finally triggered as shown in Figure 3.103. For the last couple of months, there have not been *any* trades for the EURUSD. Many people wonder how they can make a living trading if there are months when there are no trades. Remember, we are only backtesting one instrument. If you look back at what we have been doing, you will notice that we are analyzing an instrument *once*. During the analysis, we are placing bullish/bearish alert/entries. Once the entry or the alert triggers, we then go back to that instrument. Until the alert/entry is triggered, we *do not* go back to that instrument at all. Therefore, if you are analyzing and setting up alerts for each instrument, you should be able to support trading multiple instruments.

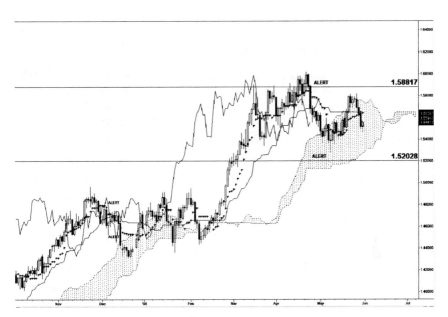

FIGURE 3.102 TradeStation Daily Ichimoku Chart of EURUSD May 30, 2008

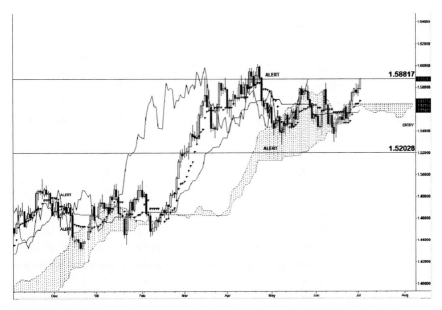

FIGURE 3.103 TradeStation Daily Ichimoku Chart of EURUSD July 2, 2008

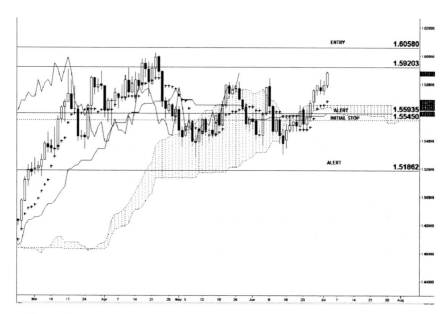

FIGURE 3.104   TradeStation Daily Ichimoku Chart of EURUSD July 2, 2008

In Figure 3.104 you can see the entry values. Notice that the entry is too far from Kijun Sen. Therefore, we cannot enter yet. Some may say why did you choose an entry so high? The entry was the buffer above the *last* high. Any value below the last high really did not fit our trading plan. If the alert had triggered a couple of days before July 2, 2008, we could have possibly chosen an entry where it would have triggered on July 2, 2008. I leave it to you to go through this exercise to see what would have happened. Figure 3.105 illustrates the new alerts.

On July 11, 2008, the bullish alert was triggered as illustrated in Figure 3.106. All the Ichimoku indicators are good for a bullish trade. However, the entry price would still be far away from the Kijun Sen. Therefore, we have to hold off for a trade entry. We will reset our alerts and move forward with the backtest (Figure 3.107).

On July 15, 2008, the bullish alert was triggered as illustrated in Figure 3.108. Currently, the Kijun Sen is 1.5670 and a possible entry would be 1.6078. This is more than 300 pips away. Therefore, all we need to do is reset our alerts and move forward with the backtest (Figure 3.109).

On July 30, 2008, the bearish alert was triggered (Figure 3.110). Some may be wondering why we chose the bearish alert where we did. Why was it not lower? That is a valid question and Figure 3.111 explains exactly why on the charts.

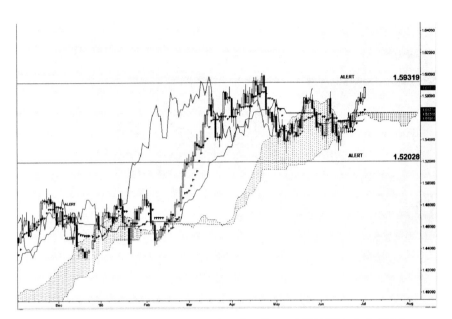

FIGURE 3.105 TradeStation Daily Ichimoku Chart of EURUSD July 2, 2008

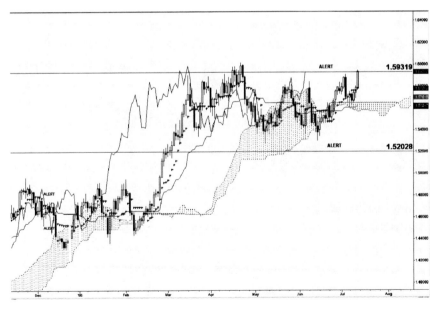

FIGURE 3.106 TradeStation Daily Ichimoku Chart of EURUSD July 11, 2008

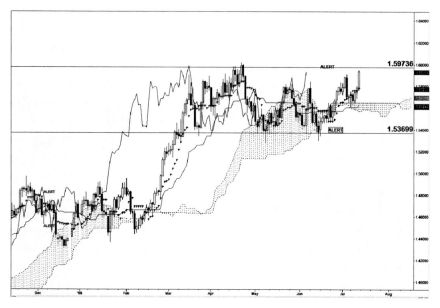

FIGURE 3.107   TradeStation Daily Ichimoku Chart of EURUSD July 11, 2008

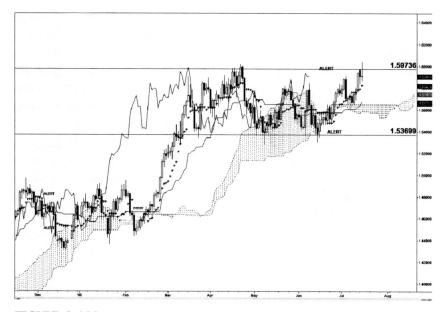

FIGURE 3.108   TradeStation Daily Ichimoku Chart of EURUSD July 15, 2008

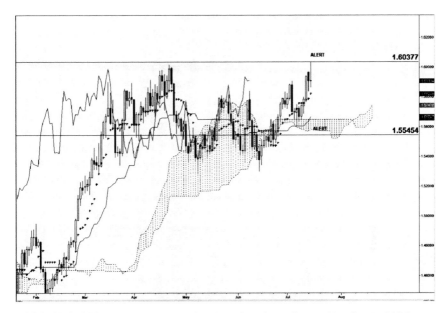

FIGURE 3.109 TradeStation Daily Ichimoku Chart of EURUSD July 15, 2008

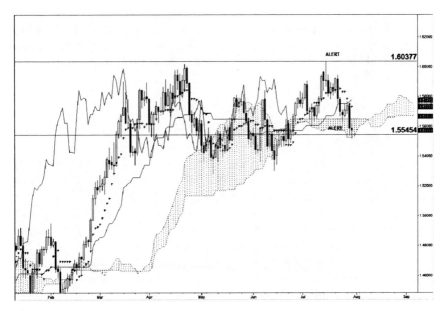

FIGURE 3.110 TradeStation Daily Ichimoku Chart of EURUSD July 30, 2008

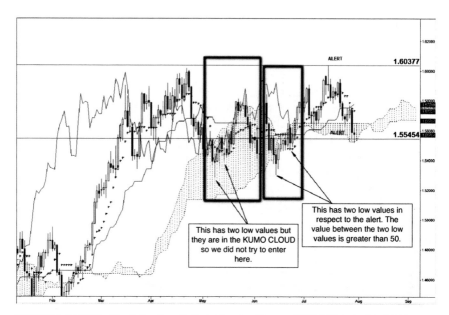

FIGURE 3.111 TradeStation Daily Ichimoku Chart of EURUSD July 30, 2008

According to the charts in Figure 3.112, we still cannot place an order entry. The reason is that price is 340 from the Kijun Sen, which is outside our trading plan limits. Therefore, we will reset our alerts and move forward (Figure 3.113).

On August 6, 2008, the bearish alert was triggered (Figure 3.114). The Ichimoku indicators are good for a bearish trade. The price versus Kijun Sen distance, which has been the problem most of the time, is a problem again. We need it to equalize more so we will wait a little while longer. The alerts have been reset and shown in Figure 3.115.

On August 7, 2008, the bearish alert was triggered (Figure 3.116). In examining the Ichimoku indicators, we are set to enter a bearish trade. However, price is still more than 300 pips away from Kijun Sen so we cannot enter. Notice that the Kijun Sen is pointing downward along with the Tenkan Sen even with the far distance between price and Kijun Sen. We will set up the alerts and move forward (Figure 3.117).

On August 8, 2008, price moved down drastically and triggered our bearish alert (Figure 3.118). We have not been able to enter the trade because of price distance from Kijun Sen and now this distance as gone further. Maybe we should have opened up the distance when Kijun Sen and Tenkan Sen pointed in the same direction of the trend. We can put this down as an optimization and try it later. For now, we have an active

FIGURE 3.112 TradeStation Daily Ichimoku Chart of EURUSD July 30, 2008

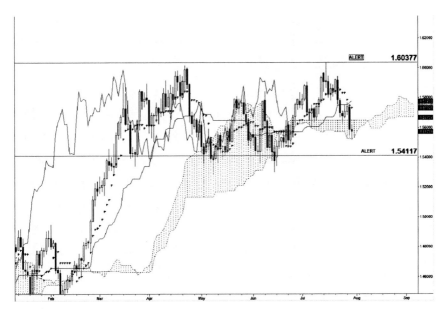

FIGURE 3.113 TradeStation Daily Ichimoku Chart of EURUSD July 30, 2008

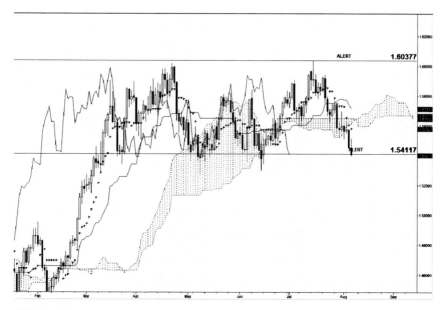

FIGURE 3.114   TradeStation Daily Ichimoku Chart of EURUSD Aug 6, 2008

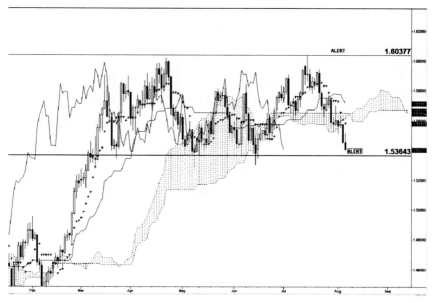

FIGURE 3.115   TradeStation Daily Ichimoku Chart of EURUSD Aug 6, 2008

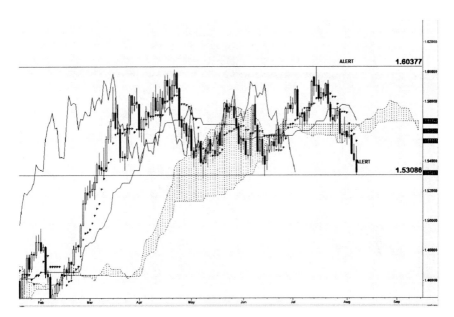

FIGURE 3.116 TradeStation Daily Ichimoku Chart of EURUSD Aug 7, 2008

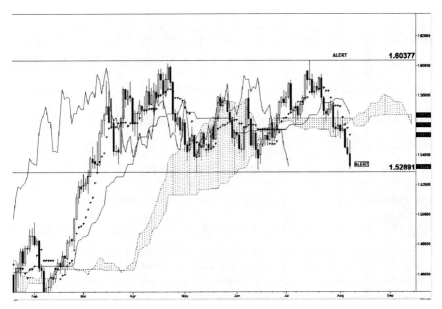

FIGURE 3.117 TradeStation Daily Ichimoku Chart of EURUSD Aug 7, 2008

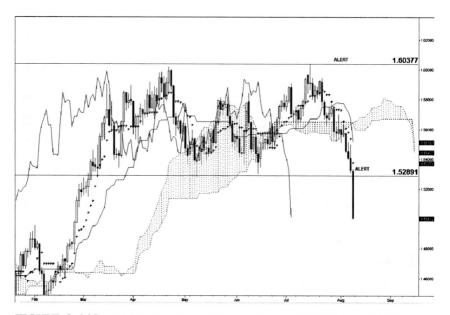

FIGURE 3.118   TradeStation Daily Ichimoku Chart of EURUSD Aug 8, 2008

trading plan and we need to keep on moving. Therefore, we will reset the alerts and they are illustrated in Figure 3.119.

Figure 3.120 shows that the alert was triggered on August 11, 2008 and illustrates that we missed the big move. As a result, we are going to drastically move the bearish alert down so it does not get triggered yet as shown in Figure 3.121. It is dangerous to get into a trend that has already drastically moved. You can enter the trend trade on a major pullback which is what we will try to do.

Figure 3.122 shows the Ichimoku chart on September 1, 2008. The chart now shows that a possible pullback may be coming very soon. We do not know if it will be a minor pullback or a major pullback. Only time will give us this answer.

On September 26, 2008, we were finally able to set the bearish alert. Figure 3.123 illustrates the chart with the two alerts. We have chosen the bearish alert at the Kijun Sen. Since price has gone above Kijun Sen, two scenarios now exist. Either the trend has reversed or a major pullback is occurring. Due to the drastic movement downward, there is a high probability that profit taking is occurring so you have a major pullback. When the trend continues, price will have to cross over the Kijun Sen so we are setting up an alert at that location.

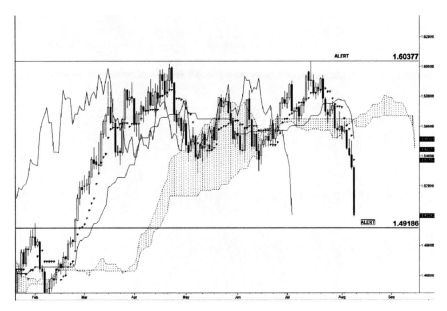

FIGURE 3.119 TradeStation Daily Ichimoku Chart of EURUSD Aug 8, 2008

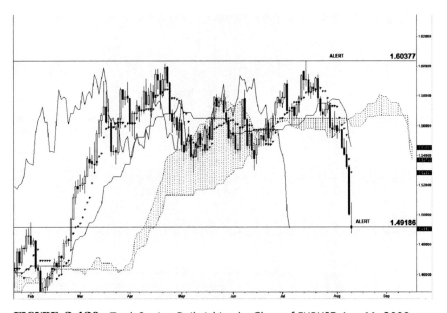

FIGURE 3.120 TradeStation Daily Ichimoku Chart of EURUSD Aug 11, 2008

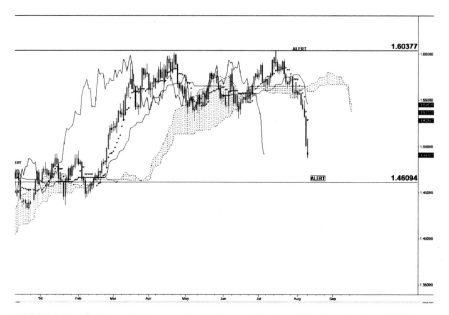

FIGURE 3.121 TradeStation Daily Ichimoku Chart of EURUSD Aug 11, 2008

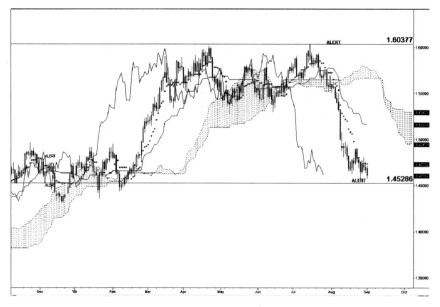

FIGURE 3.122 TradeStation Daily Ichimoku Chart of EURUSD Sept 1, 2008

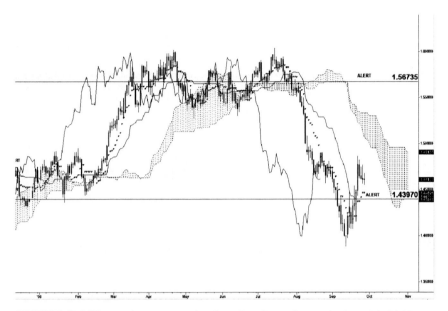

FIGURE 3.123 TradeStation Daily Ichimoku Chart of EURUSD Sept 26, 2008

On September 29, 2008, the bearish alert has triggered (Figure 3.124). In examining the Ichimoku indicators we have noticed:

- A drastic move down will cause Tenkan Sen and Kijun Sen to cross into a bearish scenario.
- Chikou is getting close to price but still has a chance to move away from price if the movement down occurs very soon. Therefore, if our entry "sits out" there for a while, we will change it to an alert again.
- Kumo Future is still healthy and the cloud has thinned out a little.
- Kijun Sen is pointing down.

Figure 3.125 shows the entry setup for the trade.

On September 30, 2008, we entered the bearish trade (Figure 3.126). Price gapped down hard so that it got us to Preserve mode right away. This means we should now start to use the Tenkan Sen as a stop. However, there is one problem and that is the Tenkan Sen is higher than the Kijun Sen so the Kijun Sen is a tighter stop for now. Therefore, we will use the Kijun Sen as a stop until Tenkan Sen and Kijun Sen cross over. The entry statistics are shown in Table 3.18.

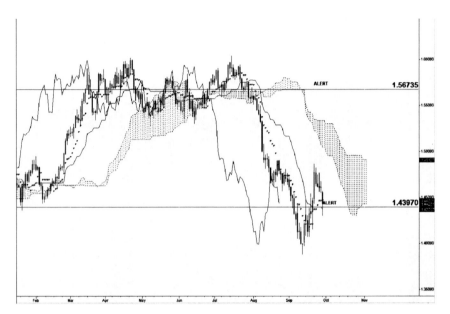

FIGURE 3.124 TradeStation Daily Ichimoku Chart of EURUSD Sept 29, 2008

FIGURE 3.125 TradeStation Daily Ichimoku Chart of EURUSD Sept 29, 2008

FIGURE 3.126 TradeStation Daily Ichimoku Chart of EURUSD Sept 30, 2008

On October 14, 2008, we were stopped out of our bearish trade with a profit. Figure 3.127 shows the chart with all the values. The exit statistics are shown in Table 3.19.

In Figure 3.128, we have shown the new alerts for EURUSD for October 14, 2008.

On October 16, 2008, the bearish alert was triggered (Figure 3.129). The Ichimoku indicators look good but the distance between price and Kijun Sen is too huge. Therefore, we reset our alerts and wait (Figure 3.130).

Figure 3.131 shows the Ichimoku chart on October 20, 2008. We got very close to hitting our alert but it did not trigger.

TABLE 3.18 Entry Trade Statistics for EURUSD on Sept 30, 2008, Trade #8

Statistics	Value
Entry Date	Sept 30, 2008
Entry Price	1.4266
Entry Stop	1.4508
Entry Risk	242 pips

FIGURE 3.127 TradeStation Daily Ichimoku Chart of EURUSD Oct 14, 2008

On October 21, 2008, our bearish alert was triggered again (Figure 3.132). Just like before, price is still far from the Kijun Sen so we have to move on with our alerts.

Figure 3.133 shows that we have moved forward to November 28, 2008, in our backtest. Between October and November, we had many opportunities to set up short entries but we kept on running into the same issue over

TABLE 3.19 Trade Statistics for EURUSD on Oct 14, 2008, Trade #8

Statistics	Value
Entry Date	Sept 30, 2008
Exit Date	Oct 14, 2008
Entry Price	1.4266
Exit Price	1.3750
Entry Stop	1.4508
Entry Risk	242 pips
Profit	$1.4266 - 1.3750 = 516$ pips
Max Profits	$1.4266 - 1.3257 = 1009$
Max Drawdown	N/A
Risk/Reward	0.47

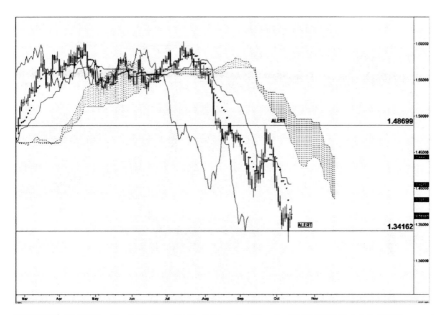

FIGURE 3.128 TradeStation Daily Ichimoku Chart of EURUSD Oct 14, 2008

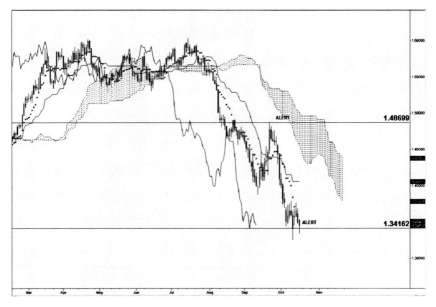

FIGURE 3.129 TradeStation Daily Ichimoku Chart of EURUSD Oct 16, 2008

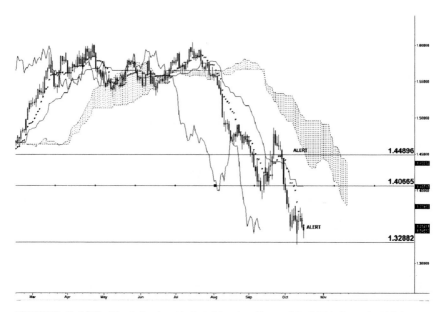

FIGURE 3.130 TradeStation Daily Ichimoku Chart of EURUSD Oct 16, 2008

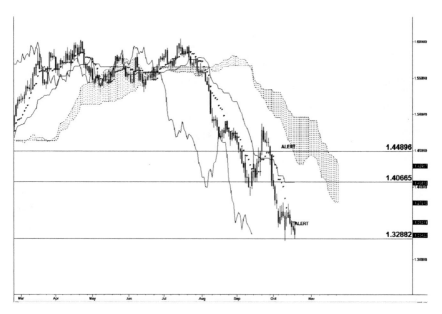

FIGURE 3.131 TradeStation Daily Ichimoku Chart of EURUSD Oct 20, 2008

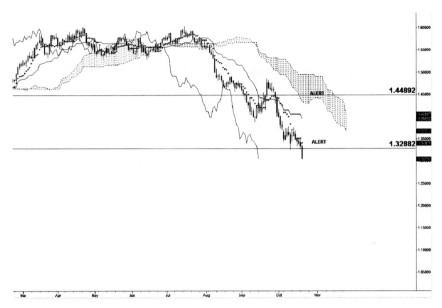

FIGURE 3.132 TradeStation Daily Ichimoku Chart of EURUSD Oct 21, 2008

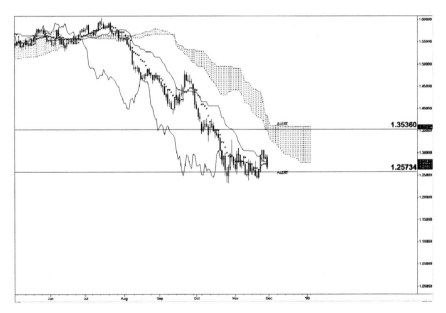

FIGURE 3.133 TradeStation Daily Ichimoku Chart of EURUSD Nov 28, 2008

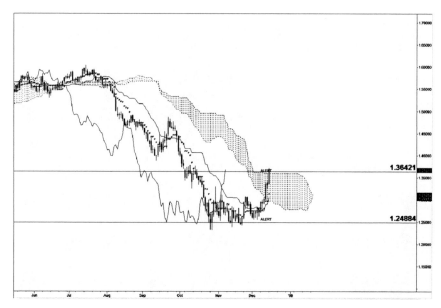

FIGURE 3.134   TradeStation Daily Ichimoku Chart of EURUSD Dec 15, 2008

and over. This issue was that price was too far away from the Kijun Sen. In other words, it was greater than 300 pips.

Figure 3.134 illustrates a chart where the bullish alerts have been triggered. The analysis of the Ichimoku indicators shows the following:

- Both Tenkan Sen and Kijun Sen are in a thick cloud, which causes consolidation.
- Kumo Future Cloud is neutral.
- Chikou Span is in "open space."

Not all the Ichimoku indicators are ideal so we will have to reset the alerts and wait.

The chart in Figure 3.135 looks ideal to set up a bullish entry. However, price is too far from the Kijun Sen.

SUMMARY—TWO YEARS OF BACKTESTING

You now have gone through two years of a backtest for the EURUSD with a particular trading plan. The trading plan we used is the first basic trading

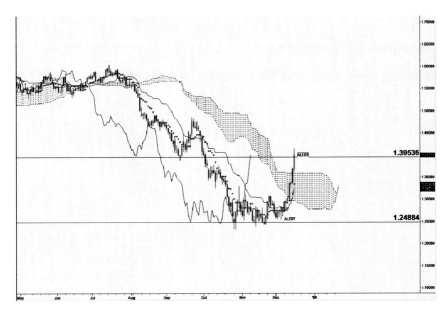

FIGURE 3.135 TradeStation Daily Ichimoku Chart of EURUSD Dec 16, 2008

plan. It allows us to have a profitable two years. There are many different optimization techniques we can try to increase the profit drastically. In fact, if you think about it, there was one rule that kept us out of many major profits. The rule was where Kijun Sen and price have to be within 300 pips of each other. If this rule can be altered, we may be able to double our profits over the two years' historical backtest.

## CHAPTER 4

Post-Analysis

T he post-analysis section is one of the key sections for backtesting. It gives the trader the "complete picture" on the trading plan that was used for the backtest. The goal of the analysis is to analyze the results for a particular backtest period. From the results and also the backtest, you can derive ways to change the trading plan in order to increase profits, increase risk/reward ratio, and so forth.

In this chapter, we take you through the step-by-step process of examining the backtest results and then begin to go through *some* optimization scenarios. There are many different things you can try so we do not say that we complete the optimization because that word really does not exist here. Markets change daily so there is no complete answer. We have to adapt to the market, otherwise it will eliminate us.

EXAMINING THE BACKTEST RESULTS

With the current trading plan, Table 4.1 shows the trades that we entered.

Table 4.1 shows the complete statistics for all eight trades from January 1, 2007, to January 1, 2009, for the daily time frame for the instrument EURUSD. We were profitable so that is a good *first* start. The problem you should see right away with this trading plan is that there was a lot of risk compared to profits. In other words the risk/reward ratio was 1.51. The goals of a trend system are to minimize losses when you are wrong and maximize profits when you are right. It matters when one loss can

TABLE 4.1 Original Ichimoku Trading Plan Results

#	Entry Date	Entry Price	Entry Risk	Exit Date	Exit Price	Max Profit	Max Drawdown	50% Max Profit	Profit	Risk/Reward
1	2/27/07	1.3236	210	5/2/07	1.3570	445	164	Y	334	0.63
2	7/10/07	1.3720	267	8/9/07	1.3669	131	112	N/A	−51	N/A
3	9/12/07	1.3891	297	10/3/07	1.4120	389	64	Y	229	1.30
4	10/19/07	1.4318	276	11/12/07	1.4537	431	149	Y	219	1.26
5	11/20/07	1.4791	343	11/20/07	1.4838	47	61	Y	47	7.29
6	2/27/08	1.5025	274	3/20/08	1.5553	878	—	Y	528	0.52
7	4/16/08	1.5955	340	4/24/08	1.5955	63	N/A	Y	−315	N/A
8	09/30/08	1.4266	242	10/14/08	1.3750	1,009	—		516	0.47
	TOTAL		2,249			3,423			1,507	1.51

TABLE 4.2 Adjustments Needed to Ichimoku Trade Plan, Include Entry Buffer

Bullish Entry Rules

Entry Price has to be less than 300 pips from the Kijun Sen + Entry Buffer. If not, you have to wait for it to equalize and come back into range.

Entry Price has to be more than 300 pips from the Kijun Sen − Entry Buffer. If not, you have to wait for it to equalize and come back into range.

"overpower" more than one-win profits. With the risk/reward ratio of 1.51 that *can* happen. Therefore, the ratio needs to be below 1.00, otherwise you are taking too much risk. Many people gauge a trading plan by winning trades versus losing trades. Do you think this is true? Can you believe that a system can be only 40 percent correct but can produce huge profits? Is that unusual? In the last chapter of the book, we discuss this further. Believe it or not, the winning percentage really does not matter. It is the amount of profit that winning trades produce compared to the amount of losses from the losing trades.

Now that we have the final results of our backtest in an organized manner as shown in Table 4.1, we can concentrate on our goal: *Maximize profits and minimize losses*. The first task we take on is to minimize our losses. We had two losses in our original trading plan. The first is −51 and the second is −315. The loss of 315 is 21 percent of 1,501, the total profit. This is a huge number compared to the two-year profit. We need to do one of three things here. The first is to turn the loss into a profit. For that trade, the max profit is only 63. This is not much, so this first option does not look feasible. The second option is to eliminate the loss completely.

Our trading plan was focused on keeping our maximum loss per trade to 300 pips. This trade had an entry risk of 340 pips, which is above the 300-pip value. This was due to the entry buffer. We allowed the trade because our trading plan did not include the buffer in the bullish and bearish rule. If we adjust our trading plan to include the entry buffer on the rule then we can eliminate the trade completely. Table 4.2 shows the trading plan rule change for both the bearish and bullish side. Table 4.3 shows the results of the two-year backtest after the trading plan rule change. We achieved our goal of eliminating the trade completely. It added more than 200 pips to our two-year profit and reduced our risk/reward ratio below 1.0. The second option worked out really well. The third option is to minimize the loss. I really cannot think of any way we can reduce this loss so this option does not exist.

TABLE 4.3 Compare Entry Risk to 300 Pips Instead of Kijun Sen Only

#	Entry Date	Entry Price	Entry Risk	Exit Date	Exit Price	Max Profit	Max Drawdown	50% Max Profit	Profit	Risk/Reward
1	2/27/07	1.3236	210	5/2/07	1.3570	445	164	Y	334	0.63
2	7/10/07	1.3720	267	8/9/07	1.3669	131	112	N/A	−51	N/A
3	9/12/07	1.3891	297	10/3/07	1.4120	389	64	Y	229	1.30
4	10/19/07	1.4318	276	11/12/07	1.4537	431	149	Y	219	1.26
5	2/27/08	1.5025	274	3/20/08	1.5553	878	—	Y	528	0.52
6	09/30/08	1.4266	242	10/14/08	1.3750	1,009	—		516	0.47
	TOTAL		1,566			3,283			1,775	0.88

Minimizing losses was a task that we could determine quickly because we only had one big loss. If we had a couple of big losses, it would take longer to determine the cause. In actuality, before we try to minimize our losses or maximize our profits, we really need to make sure that we have a complete dataset of trades. In another words, we needed to make sure that a trading plan rule did not eliminate some good trades. A good way to do this is to look for "holes" in consistency among the trades in Table 4.1.

If you look at the results in Table 4.1, you will notice that there was a trade at least every two months until May 2008. After May 2008, we did not make a trade until September. This did not fit the normal sequence of a trade every two months. Therefore, we need to find out why because there could be some really good trades during this time period. If this time period shows consolidation then there will be no good trades. However, if the charts illustrate that it was a trending period, than there is a rule that is inhibiting the good trend trades.

If you go back through the backtest chapter, from May 2008 to September 2008 there were many opportunities to trade but we never entered any because of the one-trade plan rule. The rule that kept us out of trading a majority of the time during this time period is where the distance from price to the Kijun Sen was more than 300 pips. Therefore, the optimization we are going to try is to eliminate this rule from the trading plan on both the bullish and the bearish side. With this new trade plan, we need to backtest the daily time frame of EURUSD again from January 1, 2007, to January 1, 2008. Table 4.4 shows the backtest rules for the trading plan that eliminated the maximum 300-pip distance between price and Kijun Sen. Table 4.4 shows the following changes to the results:

- Four new trades.
- Maximum profit has almost doubled with the four new trades.
- Profit has increased with the four new trades.
- Risk/Reward has increased with the four new trades.

With this rule change, we now have a complete dataset for all the trades during a trend period. Now we can start to look at minimizing our losses and maximizing our profits. We first start by minimizing our losses because losses need to be addressed before looking at the winning trades. We minimized our losses before by changing the trading plan according to Table 4.2. However, we really cannot do that now because we eliminated that rule completely. After looking at the results in Table 4.4, we noticed that the max drawdown was 221. Therefore, we can reduce our entry risk completely. Let us alter our trading plan to now include a maximum entry risk of 250 pips. Table 4.5 shows the new backtest results.

TABLE 4.4 Eliminate 300-Pip Distance Rule from KS

#	Entry Date	Entry Price	Entry Risk	Exit Date	Exit Price	Max Profit	Max Drawdown	50% Max Profit	Profit	Risk/Reward
1	2/27/07	1.3236	210	5/2/07	1.3570	445	164	Y	334	0.63
2	7/10/07	1.3720	267	8/9/07	1.3669	131	112	N/A	−51	N/A
3	9/12/07	1.3891	297	10/3/07	1.4120	389	64	Y	229	1.30
4	10/19/07	1.4318	276	11/12/07	1.4537	431	149	Y	219	1.26
5	11/20/07	1.4791	343	12/05/07	1.4630	173	—		−161	
6	2/27/08	1.5025	274	3/20/08	1.5553	878	N/A	Y	528	0.52
7	4/16/08	1.5955	340	4/24/08	1.5955	63	N/A	Y	−315	N/A
8	08/08/08	1.5243	315	08/22/08	1.4896	616	N/A	Y	347	0.91
9	08/26/08	1.4590	706	09/15/08	1.4288	703	221	N	302	2.34
10	09/30/08	1.4266	242	10/14/08	1.3750	1,009	—	Y	516	0.47
11	10/21/08	1.3217	731	10/29/08	1.2962	886	N/A	N	255	2.87
	TOTAL		4,001			5,724			2,203	1.82

TABLE 4.5 Eliminate 300-Pip Distance Rule from KS Rule and Add Max Risk of 250 Pips

#	Entry Date	Entry Price	Entry Risk	Exit Date	Exit Price	Max Profit	Max Drawdown	50% Max Profit	Profit	Risk/Reward
1	2/27/07	1.3236	210	5/2/07	1.3570	445	164	Y	334	0.63
2	7/10/07	1.3720	250	8/9/07	1.3669	131	112	N/A	−51	N/A
3	9/12/07	1.3891	250	10/3/07	1.4120	389	64	Y	229	1.30
4	10/19/07	1.4318	250	11/12/07	1.4537	431	149	Y	219	1.26
5	11/20/07	1.4791	250	12/05/07	1.4630	173	—		−161	
6	2/27/08	1.5025	250	3/20/08	1.5553	878	—	Y	528	0.52
7	4/16/08	1.5955	250		1.5955	63	N/A	Y	−250	N/A
8	08/08/08	1.5243	250	08/22/08	1.4896	616	N/A	Y	347	0.91
9	08/26/08	1.4590	250	09/15/08	1.4288	703	221	N	302	2.34
10	09/30/08	1.4266	242	10/14/08	1.3750	1,009	—	Y	516	0.47
11	10/21/08	1.3217	250	10/29/08	1.2962	886	N/A	N	255	2.87
	TOTAL		2,702			5,724			2,268	1.19

143

We have reduced our risk without altering our trading plan drastically. Now we are going to determine how to maximize our profits. In examining Table 4.5, we observed the results in the Max Profit, the Profit, and Risk/Reward columns. There were many trades that got to a minimum of 550 pips but we "claimed" much less than that value. Therefore, we are going to add the following rule to our trading plan: If a 550-pip profit is achieved, exit the trade. Table 4.6 shows the results with the 300 Kijun Sen and price distance rule eliminated. Please note: Instead of backtesting everything again with the new rules, we are going to estimate the results. If the results look good then we will backtest it. This is why you do not have any exit dates for some trades. This is not 100 percent accurate because we exit out at a profit of 550 and more trades could exist now because we can reenter.

Table 4.7 shows the results of the 300 Kijun Sen and price distance rule eliminated, max entry risk of 250 pips, and exit the trade with profit of 550. If you compare the results from Table 4.1 to Table 4.7, you will notice that we have doubled our profits and reduced our risk/reward ratio by half. Now we have to backtest with this new trading plan to make sure the actual backtest results match the estimated backtest results. We leave you to backtest everything again and verify your results on our web site www.eiicapital.com.

Our optimization has worked really well. Just think that this is just the beginning of the optimization. There are many other things you can try. Here is a list of seven of them:

1. Increase the Preserve value from 300 to 350, 400, 450, 500.
2. Increase the Bullish Exit buffer to 50, 60, 70.
3. Increase the Bearish Exit buffer to 40, 50, 60, 70.
4. If price is 200 pips away from Kijun Sen on entry, use the Tenkan Sen as a stop.
5. For continuation trend trades always use the Tenkan Sen for a stop instead of Kijun Sen.
6. Always use the Tenkan Sen as a stop.
7. Always use the Kijun Sen as a stop with no Preserve mode.

OPTIMIZE TRADING PLAN

We have now illustrated how to create a trading plan around *one* Ichimoku strategy, a strategy designed to capture trends to maximize profits when a trend occurs, and minimize losses when a trend does not occur. We have

TABLE 4.6 Eliminate 300-Pip Distance Rule from KS Rule with 550-Pip Exit Rule

#	Entry Date	Entry Price	Entry Risk	Exit Date	Exit Price	Max Profit	Max Drawdown	50% Max Profit	Profit	Risk/Reward
1	2/27/07	1.3236	210	5/2/07	1.3570	445	164	Y	334	0.63
2	7/10/07	1.3720	267	8/9/07	1.3669	131	112	N/A	−51	N/A
3	9/12/07	1.3891	297	10/3/07	1.4120	389	64	Y	229	1.30
4	10/19/07	1.4318	276	11/12/07	1.4537	431	149	Y	219	1.26
5	11/20/07	1.4791	343	12/05/07	1.4630	173			−161	
6	2/27/08	1.5025	274	—	1.5575	550	—	Y	550	0.50
7	4/16/08	1.5955	340	4/24/08	1.5955	63	N/A	Y	−315	N/A
8	08/08/08	1.5243	315		1.4693	550	N/A	Y	550	0.57
9	08/26/08	1.4590	706		1.4040	550	221	N	550	1.28
10	09/30/08	1.4266	242		1.3716	1,009	—	Y	550	0.44
11	10/21/08	1.3217	731		1.2667	886	N/A	N	550	1.33
	TOTAL		4,001			5,724			3,005	1.33

145

TABLE 4.7 Eliminate 300-Pip Distance Rule from KS with Max Risk of 250 Pips and 550 Exit

#	Entry Date	Entry Price	Entry Risk	Exit Date	Exit Price	Max Profit	Max Drawdown	50% Max Profit	Profit	Risk/Reward
1	2/27/07	1.3236	210	5/2/07	1.3570	445	164	Y	334	0.63
2	7/10/07	1.3720	250	8/9/07	1.3669	131	112	N/A	−51	N/A
3	9/12/07	1.3891	250	10/3/07	1.4120	389	64	Y	229	1.30
4	10/19/07	1.4318	250	11/12/07	1.4537	431	149	Y	219	1.26
5	11/20/07	1.4791	250	12/05/07	1.4630	173			−161	
6	2/27/08	1.5025	250		1.5575	878	—	Y	550	0.50
7	4/16/08	1.5955	250	4/24/08	1.5955	63	N/A	Y	−250	N/A
8	08/08/08	1.5243	250		1.4693	616	N/A	Y	550	0.45
9	08/26/08	1.4590	250		1.4040	703	221	N	550	0.45
10	09/30/08	1.4266	242		1.3716	1,009	—	Y	550	0.44
11	10/21/08	1.3217	250		1.2667	886	N/A	N	550	0.44
	TOTAL		2,702			5,724			3,070	0.88

146

stepped through the backtesting of the trading plan and we have shown how you can optimize the trading plan by looking at the post-analysis statistics. The final strategy that we have derived is the "foundation strategy." It is the baseline strategy because it only captures 40 percent to 50 percent of the max profit.

Through other optimization techniques, you can capture more of the max profits, further minimize losses, and maximize profits. Future books will discuss advance optimization techniques. A breakdown of four of the advanced optimization techniques we discuss in the future are:

1. Chart Patterns
2. Multi–Time Frame Analysis
3. Entry Strategies
4. Advanced Money Management (Scaling In and Out)

## CHAPTER 5

Ichimoku Strategies

In this chapter, I discuss other Ichimoku strategies. I really hesitated in including this chapter in the book at this stage because it can be destructive. What I mean by destructive is that people will not concentrate on one strategy only. They will look at all strategies at one time and try to see which one is best for them at the beginning stage of learning Ichimoku. Instead of backtesting with one strategy, they will take all the strategies and try to backtest all at once in order to see which one is the best. If someone does that, he or she is bound to fail.

If you are a new Ichimoku student, you really need to take time to understand the "ideal" strategy that was outlined in previous chapters. This strategy is the "foundation" for the other strategies. By using and understanding the "ideal" strategy, you start to understand all the Ichimoku indicators. Without going through the steps laid out in the previous chapters, there is *no way* you will be able to successfully trade the other advanced strategies. The advanced strategies are just "segments" of the "ideal" strategies with different types of rules.

Here are five of the Ichimoku strategies:

1. Ideal Ichimoku Strategy
2. Tenkan Sen/Kijun Sen Cross Strategy
3. Kijun Sen Cross Strategy
4. Kumo Cloud Breakout Strategy
5. Future Senkou Crossover Strategy

149

Each strategy has its own purpose. I briefly go through and explain each strategy and the rules behind them. Different Ichimoku traders have different rule sets for each strategy. The rule sets that are outlined are the ones that I have experience with in both historical and live trading modes.

IDEAL ICHIMOKU STRATEGY

This is the same strategy used in the previous chapters. I view this as the "highest probability" strategy because it is a safe, conservative strategy. The goal of this strategy is to get 30 percent to 40 percent of the trend. You will *not* get the beginning of the trend and most likely you will not get the end of the trend. In fact, depending on your trading plan, you will most likely get a losing trade when the trend is about to be over. This strategy uses all the Ichimoku indicators so you must understand all the indicators and how well they work together in order to trade this strategy. I also call this the "foundation strategy." Without knowing this strategy inside and out, you will not be able to understand/trade the other strategies successfully.

The basic bullish rules for this strategy are:

- Price above the Kumo Cloud.
- Tenkan Sen greater than the Kijun Sen.
- Chikou Span is greater than the price from 26 periods ago.
- Future Senkou A is greater than the Future Senkou B.
- Price is not far from Kijun Sen and Tenkan Sen.
- Tenkan Sen, Kijun Sen, and Chikou Span should not be in a thick Kumo Cloud.

The basic bearish rules for this strategy are:

- Price below the Kumo Cloud.
- Tenkan Sen less than the Kijun Sen.
- Chikou Span is less than the price from 26 periods ago.
- Future Senkou A is less than the Future Senkou B.
- Price is not far from Kijun Sen and Tenkan Sen.
- Tenkan Sen, Kijun Sen, and Chikou Span should not be in a thick Kumo Cloud.

Tenkan Sen/Kijun Sen Crossover Strategy

In the trading world, many people trade simple strategies such as 10/30 crossover strategy. The 10 is a 10 period simple moving average and the

30 is a 30 period simple moving average. Traders use this crossover in conjunction with the 200 period simple moving averages (SMA). If the 10 period SMA crosses over the 30 period SMA when price is above the 200 period SMA then a bullish trade is entered. If the 10 period SMA crosses below the 30 period SMA when price is below the 200 period SMA then a bearish trade is entered. The 200 period SMA controls the direction of the trade. This strategy has been used and traded for many years. In fact, many other strategies have been created from this one. The Tenkan Sen/Kijun Sen crossover strategy is similar to this strategy.

The basic bullish rules for this strategy are:

- Price is above the Kumo Cloud or it can be a certain distance below a nonthick Kumo Cloud. For currencies, I use a value of 50 pips below the Kumo Cloud as long as the cloud is a thin cloud. I want a thin cloud because I am assuming that price is going to go right through the cloud to the upside.
- Tenkan Sen is crossing above the Kijun Sen.
- Chikou San is in "open space."
- Price, Tenkan Sen, Kijun Sen, and Chikou should not be in the Kumo Cloud. If they are, it should be a thick cloud.
- Optional: Future Senkou A is greater than or equal to the Future Senkou B.
- Optional: Future Kumo Cloud is not thick.

The basic bearish rules for this strategy are:

- Price is below the Kumo Cloud or it can be a certain distance below a nonthick Kumo Cloud. For currencies, I use a value of 50 pips above the Kumo Cloud as long as the cloud is a thin cloud. I want a thin cloud because I am assuming that price is going to go right through the cloud to the downside.
- Tenkan Sen is crossing below the Kijun Sen.
- Chikou San is in "open space."
- Price, Tenkan Sen, Kijun Sen, and Chikou should not be in the Kumo Cloud. If they are, it should be a thick cloud.
- Optional: Future Senkou A is less than or equal to the Future Senkou B.
- Optional: Future Kumo Cloud is not thick.

Figure 5.1 shows an example of a bullish Tenkan Sen/Kijun Sen crossover. This is an interesting chart because with the "naked eye," the chart looks "ugly." Price is more than 200 pips away from the Kijun Sen and Tenkan Sen and getting ready to enter the thick Kumo Cloud. You can apply the basic rules that I provided and you will see that they are all valid

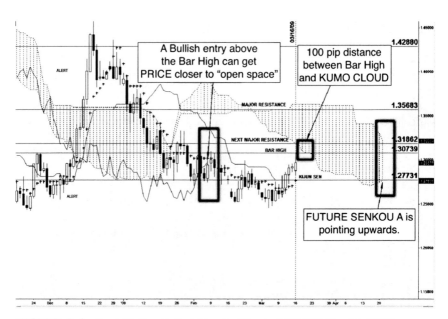

FIGURE 5.1 TradeStation Daily Ichimoku Chart of EURUSD Mar 16, 2009

for this trade. Therefore, you can set up for a bullish entry. Before you do that, you need to create a trading plan around the basic rules we provided. I have not given you any information for the trading plan such as what stops to use, what is the Preserve mode value if there is one at all, and so forth. In the previous chapter, I showed you how to create a trading plan around a strategy, backtest the trading plan, and then optimize the trading plan. For each of these advance Ichimoku strategies, this will need to be done. I will not provide you full details or an example of the trading plan for these advance strategies in this book. The reason for this is that in order to understand and use the advanced strategies, the basic strategy must be mastered. You need to learn the entire process and how to do it because nothing is "definite." Trading plans change and evolve just as markets change and evolve.

Figure 5.2 is another example of the Tenkan Sen/Kijun Sen bullish cross. This chart looks a lot "cleaner" than the previous example. All the rules are good so a bullish entry can be set up with no problems at all. Figure 5.3 shows the results of the bullish entry. Depending on your trading plan, you would either lose or gain 250 pips to 400 pips on this trade. If you used the "ideal strategy" then you would have just been a little positive. You can now see that these advanced strategies allow you to capture more of the trend. However, there are consequences for doing so. You will learn them as you backtest your trading plan with these strategies.

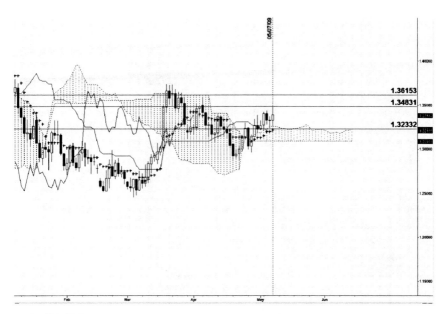

FIGURE 5.2 TradeStation Daily Ichimoku Chart of EURUSD May 7, 2009

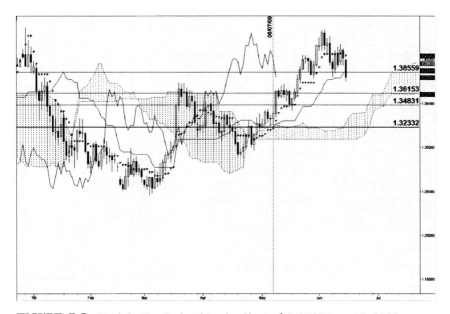

FIGURE 5.3 TradeStation Daily Ichimoku Chart of EURUSD June 15, 2009

Kijun Sen Crossover Strategy

I call this strategy the day-trading strategy. The other strategies can be used for day trading but this strategy is ideal because it has the lowest risk factor compared to all the other strategies. In order to get the lower risk factor, you have to give up something else. Can anyone guess what it is? Well, it is the probability of success. The probability of success is lower because you can get stopped out of a trade more often compared to the other strategies. The win/loss ratio for this strategy can be extremely high.

The basic bullish rules for this strategy are:

- Price cross over the Kijun Sen.
- If Tenkan Sen is less than Kijun Sen then Tenkan Sen should be pointing upward while the Kijun Sen is flat.
- Or Tenkan Sen is greater than the Kijun Sen.
- Chikou Span is in "open space."
- Future Senkou B is flat or pointing upward.
- If Future Senkou A is less than Future Senkou B then Future Senkou A must be pointing upward.
- Price, Tenkan Sen, Kijun Sen, and Chikou should not be in the Kumo Cloud. If they are, it should be a thick cloud.
- Price is not far from Tenkan Sen and Kijun Sen.
- Optional: Future Kumo Cloud is not thick.

The basic bearish rules for this strategy are:

- Price cross below the Kijun Sen.
- If Tenkan Sen is greater than Kijun Sen then Tenkan Sen should be pointing downward while the Kijun Sen is flat.
- Or Tenkan Sen is less than the Kijun Sen.
- Chikou Span is in "open space."
- Future Senkou B is flat or pointing downward.
- If Future Senkou A is greater than Future Senkou B then Future Senkou A must be pointing downward.
- Price, Tenkan Sen, Kijun Sen, and Chikou should not be in the Kumo Cloud. If they are, it should be a thick cloud.
- Price is not far from Kijun Sen and Tenkan Sen.
- Optional: Future Kumo Cloud is not thick.

Figure 5.4 is an example of the Kijun Sen cross strategy. All the conditions are true except for one—the Chikou Span. The Chikou Span is still bearish and within the Kumo Cloud. If we set up an entry above the major resistance value of 1.3615 then the Chikou Span is not an issue anymore.

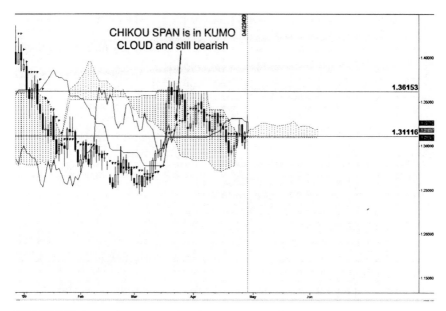

FIGURE 5.4 TradeStation Daily Ichimoku Chart of EURUSD Apr 29, 2009

Therefore, we can enter a bullish trade if our trading plan allows it. Figure 5.3 shows the results of this trade. By the time we enter this trade, the "ideal" strategy and also the Tenkan Sen/Kijun Sen strategy will be true as well. We may have a little difference on the entry price but it will not be that different.

Kumo Cloud Breakout Strategy

This strategy is my least favorite strategy. Basically, you enter a trade as soon as price breaks out of the Kumo Cloud. I do not like this strategy too much because there are many times where prices break out of the Kumo Cloud and then the next bar or bars reverse right away. It was basically a "fake" break of a major support or resistance.

The basic bullish rules for this strategy are:

- Price closes above the Kumo Cloud.
- If Tenkan Sen is less than Kijun Sen then Tenkan Sen should be pointing upward while the Kijun Sen is flat.
- Or Tenkan Sen is greater than the Kijun Sen.
- Chikou Span is in "open space."
- Future Senkou B is flat or pointing upward.

- If Future Senkou A is less than Future Senkou B then Future Senkou A must be pointing upward.
- Price, Tenkan Sen, Kijun Sen, and Chikou should not be in the Kumo Cloud. If they are, it should be a thick cloud.
- Price is not far from Tenkan Sen and Kijun Sen.
- Optional: Future Kumo Cloud is not thick.

The basic bearish rules for this strategy are:

- Price closes below the Kumo Cloud.
- If Tenkan Sen is greater than Kijun Sen then Tenkan Sen should be pointing downward while the Kijun Sen is flat.
- Or Tenkan Sen is less than the Kijun Sen.
- Chikou Span is in "open space."
- Future Senkou B is flat or pointing downward.
- If Future Senkou A is more than Future Senkou B then Future Senkou A must be pointing downward.
- Price, Tenkan Sen, Kijun Sen, and Chikou should not be in the Kumo Cloud. If they are, it should be a thick cloud.
- Price is not far from Tenkan Sen and Kijun Sen.
- Optional: Future Kumo Cloud is not thick.

Figure 5.5 shows an example of the Kumo Cloud breakout strategy. Notice that there were two breakouts that occurred for this instrument over a six-month time period. The first one was for 1,000 pips and the second was for less than 100. If you could not see the price bars after the breakout bar, do you think both breakouts look the same? The bar setup looks the same. Both breakouts had the Tenkan Sen and Kijun Sen going through the Kumo Cloud. Both had the Chikou Span in "open space." Both had a Kumo Future Cloud that was bullish. In theory, there is really no *big* difference. One was successful and the other one failed miserably. This strategy by itself is weak. If you combined this strategy with others then it is strong.

Future Senkou Crossover Strategy

This strategy is an interesting strategy. To me, it is more of a time-based strategy. You can see from the charts where the Senkou A crossed Senkou B. Therefore, you can draw a vertical timeline on that crossover point. This then signifies a possible turning point for the trend or continuation of a trend. By itself, I do not think this strategy is powerful. However, by combining it with one of the other previous strategies, it is powerful.

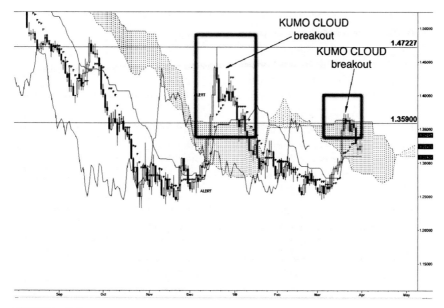

FIGURE 5.5 TradeStation Daily Ichimoku Chart of EURUSD May 1, 2009

The basic bullish rules for this strategy are:

- Current Senkou A is greater than current Senkou B.
- Price closes above the Kumo Cloud.
- If Tenkan Sen is less than Kijun Sen then Tenkan Sen should be pointing upward while the Kijun Sen is flat.
- Or Tenkan Sen is greater than the Kijun Sen.
- Chikou Span is in "open space."
- Future Senkou B is flat or pointing upward.
- If Future Senkou A is less than Future Senkou B then Future Senkou A must be pointing upward.
- Price, Tenkan Sen, Kijun Sen, and Chikou should not be in the Kumo Cloud. If they are, it should be a thick cloud.
- Price is not far from Tenkan Sen and Kijun Sen.
- Optional: Future Kumo Cloud is not thick.

The basic bearish rules for this strategy are:

- Current Senkou A is less than current Senkou B.
- Price closes below the Kumo Cloud.

- If Tenkan Sen is greater than Kijun Sen then Tenkan Sen should be pointing downward while the Kijun Sen is flat.
- Or Tenkan Sen is less than the Kijun Sen.
- Chikou Span is in "open space."
- Future Senkou B is flat or pointing downward.
- If Future Senkou A is more than Future Senkou B then Future Senkou A must be pointing downward.
- Price, Tenkan Sen, Kijun Sen, and Chikou should not be in the Kumo Cloud. If they are, it should be a thick cloud.
- Price is not far from Tenkan Sen and Kijun Sen.
- Optional: Future Kumo Cloud is not thick.

Figure 5.6 shows an example of the Senkou A and Senkou B crossover strategy. We have placed a vertical line on each cross and specified the type of crossover. Notice, none of the Senkou crossovers worked at all.

Figure 5.7 shows another example of the Senkou crossover. This time, the bullish Senkou crossover worked and it worked really well. If you observed the signals at the time of the crossover, all the other strategies showed entry signals, too. Isn't that interesting?

This brings us to an interesting point. We have now discussed all the individual strategies and what the advantages and disadvantages are for

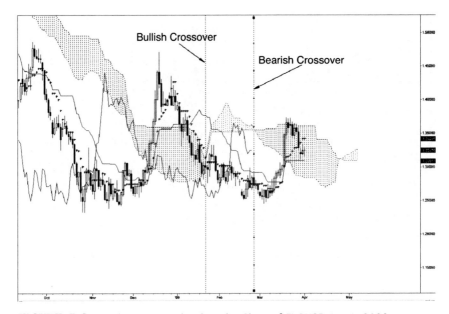

FIGURE 5.6   TradeStation Daily Ichimoku Chart of EURUSD Apr 1, 2009

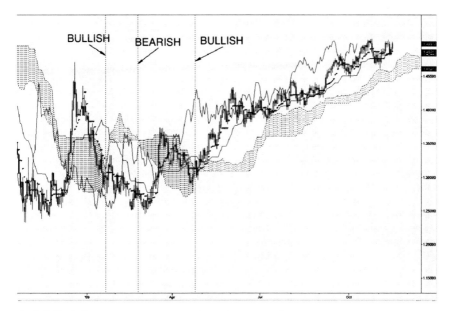

FIGURE 5.7 TradeStation Daily Ichimoku Chart of EURUSD Nov 16, 2009

each strategy. In going through each strategy, we have noticed that the high probability of success is seen when two or more strategies show entry signals in price close to each other. In Figure 5.7, the last signal had four strategies showing entry signals within four days from each other. Notice that the end result of the trade is that the trend went for over 2,000 pips over a seven-month period.

Here are some combinations of useful strategies that I use:

- Kijun Sen crossover over and then a Tenkan Sen and Kijun Sen crossover.
- Kumo Breakout Strategy and then a Tenkan Sen and Kijun Sen crossover.

## CHAPTER 6

Ichimoku Time Elements

U sually, I hesitate to discuss the time elements within Ichimoku. The reason is that it is the most complex element of Ichimoku. Also, without understanding how Ichimoku relates to price, it is difficult, if not impossible, to understand the time elements. I write about it in this book because it has been mentioned in the Ichimoku discussion forum. In my trading, *I do not* use the Ichimoku time elements. I use W.D. Gann's time elements instead. There are many similarities between the two theories but my preference is W.D. Gann. I go through a comparison of the two theories now and let you determine which one you like the most.

ICHIMOKU TIME ELEMENTS

Before you go through the discussion of the time elements, let me discuss the assumptions for the analysis. When you analyze the stock market, you have one major problem and that is whether you should include the weekends. The weekends are nontrading days. Some people include the weekends in their time estimates and some do not. There is no right or wrong answer, believe it or not. So what do you do? Well, the best thing to do is make an assumption and then base everything off it. As long as you do not change the assumption, all the research is valid. If, by chance, the assumption is changed then you will have to redo all your research.

The second assumption is that the Ichimoku time elements work mainly for the daily and weekly time frames. You can use them for lower

TABLE 6.1   Ichimoku Time
Element Value

Key Trading Number

9
17
26
33
42
51
65
76
83
97
101
129
172
200
257

time frames, but in my experience they are not too effective. Please prove it to yourself through backtests and chart analysis.

Table 6.1 describes the key Ichimoku time elements. The main numbers in the table are 9, 17, and 26. The numbers 9 and 26 originate from the Ichimoku formula of the Tenkan Sen and the Kijun Sen. All the other numbers are derived by adding and/or subtracting these numbers with other derivates of these numbers. This is a confusing statement and is best clarified by showing the exact calculations for the Ichimoku time elements. You can see these computations in Table 6.2. I cannot see a pattern on how

TABLE 6.2   Computations of the Ichimoku
Time Element Values

9	9
17	$9 + 9 - 1$
26	$9 + 9 + 9 - 1$
33	$26 + 9 - 1$
42	$26 + 17 - 1$
65	$33 + 33 - 1$
76	$26 + 26 + 26 - 2$
129	$65 + 65 - 1$
172	$65 + 42 + 42 + 26 - 3$
257	$129 + 129 - 1$

TABLE 6.3 Ichimoku Time Element
Values with Ranges

Key Trading Number	Range
9	7–11
17	13–21
26	24–28
33	30–37
42	39–46
51	56–72

these calculations were derived and have instead just accepted them and started to apply these values to the charts for various instruments.

In some articles, you will notice that people have placed ranges around the key values. For instance, the first key Ichimoku time element is 9. Some people will say the 9 is valid as long as the number is between 7 and 11. This is the range for values that make the Ichimoku time element 9 valid. Table 6.3 shows the value of ranges around the Ichimoku time elements.

Do you see the problem with the theory of ranges with the Ichimoku time elements shown in Table 6.2? If you include the ranges with the Ichimoku time element, you cover almost all the numbers. There are more numbers covered than not covered so would it not be better to analyze the numbers not covered? You will get a smaller sample size if you do that. For example, between 7 and 21, the only number not covered is 12. How does that help? It is not useful at all. Therefore, do not use a range of values around the Ichimoku time elements. You will allow only one deviation before and after the time element but that is it.

Figure 6.1 illustrates a daily chart for the EURUSD on June 16, 2009. The chart illustrates some Ichimoku time elements that were created with the values 9, 33, 43, and 66. Notice that 43 is 1 off from 42 and 66 is 1 off from 65. It is okay to accept values off by 1 from the Ichimoku time values. There is no exact science in trading so a deviation of +/– 1 is acceptable. How did you get these values? How do you use the Ichimoku time elements? Let us go through the steps one by one in order to show how the Ichimoku time element influenced time. We first start by looking at the weekly chart of the SPX on June 19, 2009, shown in Figure 6.2.

Next, place vertical lines at every price reversal. What is the definition of price reversal? A price reversal is when price shifts has reversed for minimum of two bars with higher highs or lower lows based on the direction of the price reversal. It is a tedious job but that is what needs to be

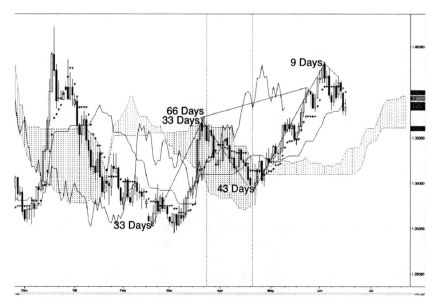

FIGURE 6.1 TradeStation Daily Ichimoku Chart of EURUSD June 16, 2009

done to learn the Ichimoku time elements. Figure 6.3 illustrates all the price reversals for a particular time period. One issue you may come across is when you have two price bars with the same high or same low at a price reversal point. Where do you place the vertical line? There is no right or wrong answer for which bar. You will have to try both and see where the

FIGURE 6.2 TradeStation Weekly Ichimoku Chart of SPX June 19, 2009

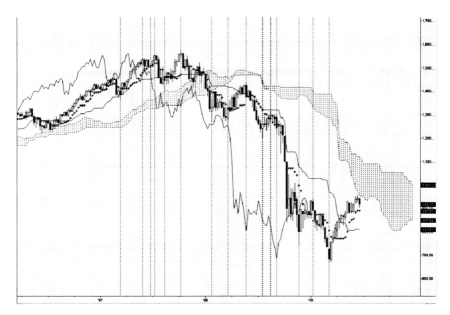

FIGURE 6.3 TradeStation Weekly Ichimoku Chart of SPX June 19, 2009

time elements fit the best. The first vertical line on the left in Figure 6.3 shows the two conflict bars.

Once the vertical lines have been placed on the chart, proceed forward in trying all the different time values between the vertical lines. I would go in sequence. What I mean is that you first need to measure the time distance between the first vertical line and the second vertical line. If the value equals one of the Ichimoku time values or is off by 1 then you keep that measurement. Next, you need to measure between the first vertical line and the third vertical line. If the value equals one of the Ichimoku time values or is off by 1 then you keep that measurement. Last, you measure between the first vertical line and the fourth vertical line. You continue doing this process over and over until you compare the first vertical line to all the other vertical lines. Keep all the measurements that equal one of the Ichimoku time values or are off by one. Now, you have completed the sequence of checking the first vertical line to all the future vertical lines (i.e., the lines to the right of the line being measured against).

Once that is done, you take the second vertical line and compute the distance value of this line with every other vertical line in the future (right). Continue to do this until all the vertical lines have been measured against all the other vertical lines. Take the time to do these measurements completely. Do not take any shortcuts. It is a tedious, repetitive task but it is something that needs to be done so you understand exactly how the time elements work for trading.

Figure 6.4 shows the results of the measurements. You may have some values I do not have but do not worry about it. There is no right or wrong answer. Notice how the price reversals matched the Ichimoku elements? The time values were accurate at the beginning of the downward trend but when the big trend occurred, over 18 weeks, there was really no match with the Ichimoku time elements. Can this happen? Yes, it can happen more often than you will believe. The time elements indicate a *possible* price reversal. Time elements by themselves are not too valuable. However, when they are combined with technical analysis, they can help drastically.

How do I use the time elements for trading? The way I use the time elements is by placing the vertical lines on my chart for all the key Ichimoku time elements from the last price reversal all the way to the Future Kumo Cloud as shown in Figure 6.5. Once the vertical lines are placed, I turn those vertical lines into alerts. This way, when the current trading date gets to one of these vertical lines, I am alerted right away. Then I go to the alerted chart and perform the technical analysis to determine if a trade exists. If a trade does not, I reset all my alerts and move on.

Figure 6.6 shows the charts for the weekly chart for SPX on July 10, 2009. Our first time alert was triggered and we examine the charts based on our technical analysis. Right now, there is no trade so we continue to move forward. Before we move on, we now have to add the time elements at the last price reversal point. We have to continue to do this at *every* price reversal point. Figure 6.7 shows the addition of the vertical lines at the previous price reversal.

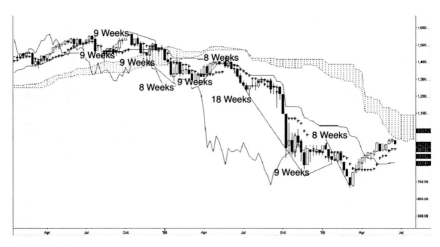

FIGURE 6.4 TradeStation Weekly Ichimoku Chart of SPX June 19, 2009

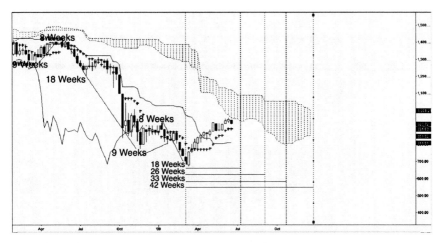

FIGURE 6.5 TradeStation Weekly Ichimoku Chart of SPX June 19, 2009

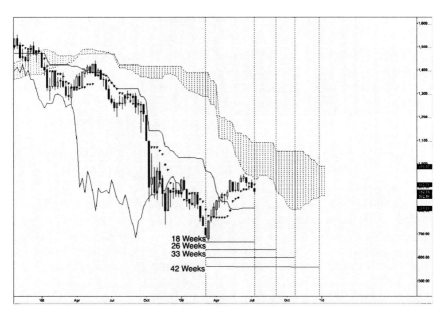

FIGURE 6.6 TradeStation Weekly Ichimoku Chart of SPX July 10, 2009

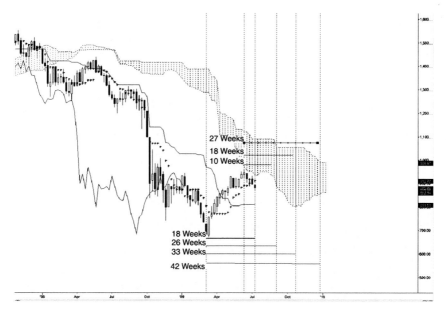

FIGURE 6.7 TradeStation Weekly Ichimoku Chart of SPX Nov 17, 2009

Figure 6.7 shows the chart for the SPX for November 17, 2009. You can see how the time elements drawn in the past have influenced price reversals in the future. This influence can be minor or major.

We use the square of odd and even numbers to get not only the proof of market movements, but the cause.

—W.D. Gann

This quote illustrates how W.D. Gann derived many of his theories. We have discussed the Ichimoku time elements in detail. Now, we briefly go through W.D. Gann time elements. There is no way we can cover every aspect of W.D. Gann's time elements in this book. There are many books and seminars on Gann's theories. In fact, it takes almost a lifetime to master all or even some parts of his theories. It took me more than two years just to get a complete understanding of some of his works. Today, we use many of his time predication calculations for future price reversals.

The time element we focus on in this book just to illustrate *some* of his theories is the square of odd numbers. Table 6.4 shows the square of odd numbers. The calculation is simple. We first square the odd numbers with each other, which is illustrated in the column to the far left. Next, we take the square of one number and subtract it from the square of the previous value. This calculation is displayed on the far right. We now have all our

TABLE 6.4 Odd Square Multiplication Table

Number	Odd Multiple	Subtract
1	1 × 1	
9	3 × 3	9 − 1 = 8
25	5 × 5	25 − 9 = 16
49	7 × 7	49 − 25 = 24
81	9 × 9	81 − 49 = 32
121	11 × 11	121 − 81 = 40
169	13 × 13	169 − 121 = 48
225	15 × 15	225 − 169 = 56
289	17 × 17	289 − 225 = 64
361	19 × 19	361 − 289 = 72
441	21 × 21	441 − 361 = 80
529	23 × 23	529 − 441 = 88
625	25 × 25	625 − 529 = 96

time elements, which indicate that a possible price reversal can take place. It is now time to apply it to the charts just like we did with the Ichimoku time elements.

Figure 6.8 shows the monthly chart of $INDU, the Dow Jones Industrial average on November 30, 2009. We have illustrated the time between the

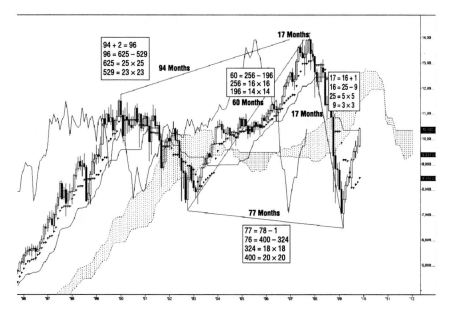

FIGURE 6.8 TradeStation Monthly Ichimoku Chart of INDU Nov 30, 2009

price reversals on a monthly basis. We can see how the values match up with the values of squared odd numbers.

This now completes the time element chapter. We now move on to the next chapter, which is probably one of the most critical chapters in this book. It deals with *you*. This chapter is actually written by a close friend of mine, Doug Laughlin. He is a good trader and offers a lot of good advice in regard to the "psychology of the mind." I honestly would take the time to read this chapter at least twice before starting to trade with live money.

## CHAPTER 7

Applied Trader Psychology

Doug Laughlin

A t this point you have learned that the Ichimoku charts and trading system can provide you with a powerful view of the markets. This view of the markets can serve as a basis for a consistent trading system that, when applied properly, can give you the tools to attack the markets whether your preference is currencies, stocks, or any other instrument that tends to have a trending component. Unfortunately, neither Ichimoku nor any other well-developed trading system can guarantee your success as a trader. The best historical trading systems have a long-term track record, a consistent trading plan, and work in multiple time frames and under different market characteristics.

The purpose of this manual is to teach you the elements of a successful trading system and its key components. The purpose of this chapter is to acknowledge and accept the given that as individual trainers we all bring with us a history of bias, emotion, and personal perception to the markets. No matter how hard we try to remain objective in trading or in life, we all bring our own perceptions, fears, opinions, and prejudices into our trading rooms. It is important that we first understand and then design methods to control these elements that we bring with us so that they do not get in the way of implementing a successful trading system.

Throughout history all of the best traders have had a well-developed system that was consistent and proven over a considerable length of time under different market conditions. None of them were great traders right out of the chute. All of them used information they had gleaned from the

171

traders that advanced before them and then fine-tuned their systems via trial and error until they ultimately found what was successful for them. You may ask at this point why not simply copy the exact system that a successful trader before you has used to their benefit? It is a valid question that deserves further consideration.

IS IT AS EASY AS JUST BEING TAUGHT A NEW SYSTEM?

Many thousands of traders over the years have tried to copy an existing system and yet for a multitude of reasons were not able to duplicate the same results. There have even been formal experiments of this nature with the best known being the well-documented Turtles trading system that was taught by Richard Dennis in the early 1980s to people off the street. He had well-documented results (supposedly he turned a $5,000 trading account into $100,000,000) and wanted to see if he could teach his system to others and see if they could get the same results. He found his new "pupils" by placing an ad in the *Wall Street Journal* and selected 14 traders to learn his system through a careful selection process.

It is for this reason that Richard Dennis wanted to train brand-new traders rather than established traders. He did not want his new pupils to bring in their own preexisting market views and biases. He simply wanted them to carefully learn his system and follow it to the letter. Traders who had already implemented their own systems and experienced their own successes and failures would have brought their own views to his system—including doubts and even creative ideas to optimize it. Ultimately his beginner pupils that originally traded his system exactly as taught would become advanced traders in their own right and would eventually customize his system to their own preferences and beliefs.

In this book that covers the nuances of the Ichimoku system there is no perfect way to trade the system. However, there are some key components that must be implemented to make it successful. From there it is up to the individual trader to fine-tune these elements and make sure the system ultimately fits his or her personal trading style. These final tweaks as applied by the trader must result in sound historical trade history to provide the conviction and success quotient necessary to allow the trader to follow the rules once the trading plan has been established.

THE PROBLEM WE HAVE WITH GETTING IN OUR OWN WAY

It should be noted that trading is not an inherent trait in us as individuals. The best systems often fly in the face of what our internal biases tell us we should be doing. We all as humans have an inherent tendency to "follow the herd" in all aspects of life. This is what creates fads and trends whether it comes to clothing, housing, use of the language itself, and just about every aspect of life. Our nature to follow the lead of others can be our worst enemy when it comes to trading—yet our instincts tell us to do it every time. This is why it is critical to have a system that has been predefined with a rigid rules set. Our basic human instincts will often tell us to do the opposite of what our system is telling us. Therefore, if we do not have the true conviction in our system that comes from historical performance, our tendency will be to abandon the system at just the wrong time and follow our instincts.

It has been written many times that more than 90 percent of traders give up after failures and look to another vocation in life to earn their incomes. Think about how amazing this is when you consider the tremendous desire the budding trader has on entering the trading business to create a living where you can work from the comfort of your own home with no boss and in total control of your own destiny. The siren song of the trader's life is truly an intoxicating dream to a large portion of the masses. Yet with such a strong desire, the failure rate is quite discouraging.

With this in mind, why do so many fail when their desire is so great? After all, each trade is a 50/50 proposition is it not? The instrument must either go up or down. That alone would imply that at least 50 percent of new traders should be successful—right? And with training you would expect that the 50 percent should improve rather quickly to a better than 50 percent success rate. You have heard the phrase before "If it was so easy—we'd all be doing it" and in fact we all would. Who would not want a life that provides a schedule of your own in the comfort of your own home earning a comfortable living all under your own control? Some might even call it the American Dream.

IS THERE A CONSPIRACY AGAINST THE SMALL TRADER?

So if you think about it this way you begin to almost feel like there is a conspiracy out there to keep us from being successful! How could so many fail in a system that has a 50/50 proposition and trainers galore and that has been in existence for more than 100 years? That has been the source of enormous frustration to the new trader for decades and continues to be true today. To this day I constantly hear from traders everywhere that "the market makers are in control" or "the only one that makes any money is the broker" or "the only ones that make any money are the big money guys." I am here to tell you that none of these conspiracies are true today and probably have never been the case. They are our own way of justifying our own inability to implement a successful trading system in an environment that we know has the basic elements necessary to allow us to be successful.

As a former leader of my own advanced trading group I was often shocked to hear some of the previous comments espoused by members of my own group that I was certain knew better than that and yet in a time of frustration would voice such opinions. Nobody wants to consider him- or herself a loser and for that matter most of us inherently do not even want to take a loss. Our society celebrates winning at all costs and extols the virtues of trying harder and doing more ("Just Do It") to make it happen! Although such philosophies may work well in many forms of life it does not fit the trading world very well at all.

Many successful people have attempted to become traders because they have built up a nice nest egg from their business successes and now they are ready to trade their account for a living as their new vocation. It is painful to them when they try to apply what worked well for them in their business life to the trading business—only to find that what worked well for them in one vocation may in fact work against them in their newfound trading career. It can be hard to swallow when you have known nothing but success and enter the brave new world of trading only to find that what should be seemingly easy is in fact the hardest thing you have ever done. We often see the same thing happen when successful business owners buy and take control of a sports franchise and try and run it like their businesses—and then they find out that their business acumen does not apply well in the sports field. Learning the trading business has many of the same implications.

It is for this reason that you must open your mind and accept the fact that "you don't know what you don't know" and so a rigid system with proven results is the only way to begin to build a successful trading business. Until you learn that, the school of hard knocks will happily teach you how to trade while your trading account disintegrates to nothing slowly but surely. And in many cases the harder you try the worse it gets.

TRADERS MYTH—SMART PEOPLE MAKE THE BEST TRADERS

In his book *Trade Your Way to Financial Freedom* author Van Tharp documents a case that involved 40 PhDs in an experiment that was meant to measure the ability of intelligent people to become good traders. In the experiment conducted by Ralph Vince, the PhD participants implemented a trial of 100 trades each in a simple computer game, which each of the participants were told that he or she would win 60 percent of the time. They were each given $1,000 and told to bet as much or as little as they desired on each of the trades. By the end of the game only two of the 40 participants had actually made more than their original $1,000 (even though they were assured a 60 percent winning percentage in advance). How could this be possible?

Optimally they should have invested the same amount with each trade and, if so, they would have all made money. However, their tendency was to double or even triple their bet after a continuous series of losing trades of three or four losers in a row. And in doing so they would consider their 60 percent winning odds almost a sure thing after so many losers and would increase their bet size. Upon losing again with the larger bet size their tendency would be to bet even bigger with the next bet to make up for the large loss. And ultimately they would end up exhausting their account with such a strategy. What these participants did not realize is that even with an assured winning percentage of 60 percent, all systems will have a series of consecutive losing trades. It is what you do when you have a series of losing trades that will often determine what kind of trader you become.

LOSING TRADES ARE ACCEPTABLE

If you have difficulty accepting losses it is important that you work on overcoming this trading handicap prior to trading significant money. Losses are a given in the trading business. They must be accepted and expected as they are part of the overall landscape. Anyone who has difficulty accepting a loss either needs to overcome this point of view or should consider another vocation in life and should let someone else manage their money. In fact once you have traded for a living you will realize that losses are simply a part of the necessary process of trading. They are neither bad nor good in and of themselves—they are just a part of the process. Once you begin to accept this you will be better prepared to develop and implement a system.

So we have already discussed the lure of the life of a full-time trader. It is important that we move beyond the dreams and desires of the trading life itself to find the system that best fits us. It is here that we all differ. Some of us prefer the action of constant trading throughout the day. Others would prefer to only make one or two trades per day if that much. At one time I used to trade a system that only required one trade per month. The frequency of your trades is not the important thing. You must find the trading frequency that best fits you.

In addition to finding the system that best suits your desires in terms of frequency—you also need to fit your trading system into existing circumstances. If you have a full-time job while also trading, it is important that you develop a system that accentuates your lifestyle and conditions. It needs to fit your life and it needs to fit your circumstances. Otherwise, you may learn the best trading system in history, but if it does not fit your situation it will almost certainly fail for you. This is one of the reasons there is no such thing as the perfect or "fail proof" system. Anyone who tells you there is, most certainly is trying to sell you something for their own benefit.

One of the many advantages of the Ichimoku system is that it can be applied to many different time frames. Therefore, you can adjust the frequency of trades to fit your schedule. It can also be applied to many different trading instruments. So once again, you can apply it to trading instruments that might best fit your schedule. I know many people who trade currencies so they can trade at night or in the early morning hours around their full-time job. However, they could just as easily execute longer term trades against stocks or ETFs if this was their desired preference. The important thing is to develop your rules and system to optimally fit your circumstances. There are likely thousands of trading systems out there that can be implemented successfully. The key for you as a trader is to develop one that has a positive expectancy and then stick with it.

Another factor that affects traders is the frequency of wins versus losses. There are many traders out there who just have a difficult time accepting a system that has frequent losers. The irony in this fact is that many of the best systems lose more often than they win. The reason they are successful systems is that the size of their winners is considerably larger than the size of their losers. If I recall correctly, the Turtles trading system of Richard Dennis would tend to exhibit more losing trades than winners (typically about 40 percent winners). However, it would provide winning trades that were particularly large in terms of the size of win and such winners would make up for several losers.

A SUCCESSFUL SYSTEM WILL FORTIFY YOUR CONVICTIONS

I recall years ago when Johnny Carson hosted the *Tonight Show* that he had a guest whom he called the "world's greatest trader." As I recall, the guest was a bit sheepish about the designation but he admitted that he made millions of dollars per year. Carson told the guest that if he were making millions per year that he must be good at picking winners and he asked the guest what kind of winning percentage he typically experienced. The guest shocked Carson when he told him that his typical winning percentage was about 42 to 43 percent overall but that he had just experienced his best year ever making millions of dollars with a winning percentage of approximately 45 percent. Carson scoffed and said that anyone should be able to achieve a rate of 50 percent and what kind of a great trader loses more than he wins as the audience began to laugh. The trader then proceeded to tell him that his winners were much larger than his losers as the laughter began to die off.

This lesson as evidenced by Carson's guest is important to us as traders. It is not how often you win—it is what you win over the long haul. You must be prepared to lose and lose often as this is simply part of trading. This is not to say that you cannot learn from your losers. You can and should learn from your losers. This is the all-important trial and error that will ultimately make you a better trader. The key is that you do not blow out your account while you learn from your losses.

You will recall that I talked earlier in the chapter about the conviction of your trades and your trading system itself. Blind conviction can be a dangerous system. There have been many thousands of traders indeed who have learned a system over the years and blindly placed a huge investment only to be taken out under adverse circumstances. Your conviction is important but it must be earned from historical testing under varying market characteristics and while being applied to the trading instrument you plan to ultimately use (stocks, currencies, etc.). This means that you will need to invest in a historical application of your system in your given instrument to know in fact whether the system will provide a positive expectancy. Anything other than this is a simple guess and is likely to have an adverse outcome.

Those who test his or her system extensively prior to implementation gain the conviction necessary to have a good idea what to expect when real trading (and losses) ensue. All trading systems have a drawdown, which represents the greatest possible potential loss to your trading account. You may have the makings of a great system but if it exhibits a maximum 40 percent loss (drawdown) in the course of historical testing this may be considerably more loss than you can stomach as a trader. Therefore, although the system may ultimately provide exceptional long-term results, it may be a terrible system for you because you cannot emotionally accept a 40 percent loss. Other systems may project a maximum downside loss of 20 percent but their upside potential may be reduced by a considerable percentage to boot.

We all have an individual pain threshold that is specific to us and that plays an important role in our life as a trader. This is one of the key reasons that the trader that trades "play money" does well in his account until he converts to "real money" using the same trading strategy and begins to lose money. We realize that once we commit real money to the trade we add the element of emotion that was missing while using paper trading money and this one difference makes all the difference in the world as to how we react once the losses begin. Emotions and trading do not go together. The emotional trader will ultimately become a losing trader—even with supposed proper techniques and knowledge. Their emotions will make them do the wrong thing at the wrong time. Remember, our instincts will tell us to follow the herd and in most circumstances following the herd will take us in the wrong direction. Famous trader Jimmy Rogers has often said he will happily take off their hands the commodities the sellers are desperate to unload and happily sell to them the items they are desperate to buy.

SELF-SABOTAGE AND HOW IT APPLIES TO YOUR TRADING

Although we all have good intentions about trading we can often also be the victims of self-sabotage because of our inner beliefs. These inner beliefs are often referred to as our subconscious. Although our conscious mind can only focus on so many things at once—typically only five to eight things— our subconscious is handling thousands of tasks at once. It is handling everything from our breathing, movement, memory, and so forth, to even critical elements such as our blood flow, all while allowing us to focus on our most critical conscious thoughts. The problem is that although we may be focused on a conscious thought, we may also be carrying an old (but still firmly in place) subconscious thought that is totally at odds.

Let us take an example. I once attended a workshop that used kinesiology and muscle testing techniques to test our internal beliefs. My sister, who is an experienced real estate investor, was asked to volunteer to test an internal belief that many of us have had over the years. While repeating the well-known phrase "Money is the root of all evil" she tested positive for this belief, which was much to her shock and dismay. As an investor she quickly recognized the downside to holding such a belief. With the assistance of our instructors over the next 20 minutes she learned how to overturn this belief and was once again tested to verify that she had eliminated this potentially harmful belief.

The problem for us as traders is that many of us have similar internal beliefs that were ingrained in us early in life—perhaps even as children— and they are still there and still alive in our subconscious. In most cases we do not realize they are there and therefore we think we have the right opinions, systems, and attitudes to be a good trader. Meanwhile, we have these internal beliefs that have never been explored—much less removed—that can and typically will serve to sabotage our results when we try to become a successful trader. Some may call these self-destructive traits. But they are really just incongruent beliefs that we hold inside to (in many cases) protect us from what we fear will be harmful to us, that is, becoming evil by having too much money. Think about some of the phrases we use in society such as "filthy rich" and how our politicians make us feel that the big breadwinners are somehow responsible for the circumstances of the downtrodden in some sort of a conspiratorial manner. It is no wonder that we have internal beliefs that can get in our way of successful trading.

One interesting case was that of a trader who tended to always top out at $80,000 annually and once he reached that level in a year he began losing for no apparent reason. With assistance from counseling he eventually uncovered the realization that he had always revered his father and considered him to be the finest man on earth. On further investigation it was discovered that his father's highest income ever had been about $80,000 in a year. The son later realized that he felt he was not worth more than his father and so that whenever he approached his father's peak earnings he was subconsciously sabotaging his own trading because he did not feel his worth could ever be greater than the great man he had always admired. With assistance he learned to accept and embrace the idea that it was okay for him to earn more than his father and from there he began to earn considerably more than $80,000 per year using the same techniques he had used in the past.

It is not my goal in this chapter to teach you the techniques to discover and eventually replace your internal belief systems. There are several groups and practices available to assist you with the tools and techniques to uncover and even change these beliefs. One group that specializes in these methods is a group known as Psych-K. There are others that are exploring and working in these directions using techniques ranging from NLP (neuro-linguistic programming) to hypnotic methods and even regression therapy. There are also a myriad of training coaches like the aforementioned Van Tharp to Adrienne Toghraie who can assist traders with many aspects of trader psychology.

IN SUMMARY—TRADER PSYCHOLOGY OVERALL

What I want you to gain from this understanding is that your trading results are a combination of a solid trading system that best fits your needs and trading style along with a healthy conviction for a system that you know has been tested and is successful. You must then combine that with a healthy conscious and unconscious belief system to assure your positive trading development. The author of this book, Manesh Patel, encourages you to backtest your system including entries, triggers, and exits to ensure that you have developed a successful system that fits your personality and circumstances. He gives you example systems that you can use to spur you on to develop a system that will fit you optimally.

I suggest that once you develop your system it is crucial for you to maintain a log of all your trades. Make sure you log along with each trade *why* you made the trade once you entered and then record why you exited the trade when you did. Pay particular attention to your losing trades. You will sometimes have losers simply because of market conditions that are not under your control. I have heard some experienced traders call these "good losers." And then you will likely notice you have other losing trades where you did not follow your system. It is these trades with which you need to focus extra attention. You may find a definite trend with such trades that will ultimately lead you to uncover harmful beliefs you are holding that are getting in your way of becoming a successful trader. Once acknowledged, you are well on your way to uncovering and then correcting these harmful trades that are getting in your way of accomplishing your ultimate desired success as a trader. I recommend that you continue to maintain such a log hereafter as a trader as you continue to uncover other such "glass ceilings" that can become barriers to your continuing development as a trader.

## CHAPTER 8

Day Trading
with Ichimoku

This chapter is probably the "deadliest" chapter. Most people will probably skip straight to this chapter and start to use it in a live account right away. Today, day trading is associated with "quick cash." People may hear success stories of how someone took $5,000 and turned it into $1.2 million in one year. Through the concept of margin, people now have the chance to "go to the moon" or sink to the "ocean floor" in a short amount of time.

Before I begin this chapter, let me go through a story of one of my ex-Ichimoku students. Back in 2006, I was teaching an Ichimoku class in Atlanta, Georgia. I had an enthusiastic student who guaranteed me that he would be the best Ichimoku student I ever had. He was an engineer who was eager to leave his "job." The job was demanding many hours with little pay.

Most people who have a "job" can relate to how this student was feeling. This is a typical scenario for an employee in the corporate world. A corporation's mission statement typically is "work more and pay less." This generates more revenue and keep costs drastically down so profits are great. I lived it for 16 years in the corporate world of telecommunications. The majority of people who are employed get to age 65 and realize that they have nothing because the inflation rate was increasing at a higher rate than their money market savings account. If you do not believe me, look back in history. Back in 1970, one parent's income was sufficient for the entire household. Now, both parents *have* to work and many still are living paycheck to paycheck. Look at how many day-care centers there were in the 1970s compared to now.

The reason why I am talking about this is that there are many people who turn to trading to escape the vicious "job" cycle. They do not want to live paycheck to paycheck. They want to get to a point where they do not have to worry about money now or even in the future. As a result, they turn to trading but it is not long-term trading, it is instead *day trading*. Their concept of day trading is where they can make some quick cash for investing little money (i.e., small risk). They want to be the next overnight success story. Unfortunately, this is a rare case. In fact, it is a proven fact that if a beginning trader is successful on his or her first trade, they will lose all their invested money. Why you may ask? The first successful trade is a "false sense of hope." It makes beginner traders feel like they cannot lose to a point where they start to invest more and more money. Some, in fact, invest money they do not have at all. At some point, their luck runs out and now they are leveraged high to a point where one bad move wipes out *everything*. Have you heard of any of these stories? No? Read the following story.

"*A year ago*, Craig Mazeska, a teacher at a small school for developmentally disabled children near Baltimore, was living proof that anyone with enough nerve could get rich trading stocks online.

Like the truck driver in that early Discover brokerage advertisement, Mazeska had become an unlikely millionaire almost overnight. In just four years, Mazeska, now 30 years old, parlayed an initial $20,000 investment into a portfolio worth more than $2.2 million. His hot hand allowed him to buy a two-bedroom condominium in suburban Baltimore and a BMW sports car—with cash. Some acquaintances even suggested that he consider quitting his teaching job and simply trade stocks.

It is a good thing he did not follow their advice. Since last year's violent tech sell-off, Mazeska's portfolio has been sliced to $420,000. Hey, he's still well ahead of the game, right? In fact, the situation is far worse than it appears. Mazeska owes the Internal Revenue Service more than $350,000 in unpaid taxes stemming from his huge trading gains of 1999. His once-giddy dreams of an early retirement have given way to the bitter reality of staying one step ahead of bankruptcy. These days, he and his attorney spend a lot of time trying to keep the tax man at bay without having to liquidate his entire portfolio.

"I went from this state of euphoria where I could have easily retired, to a point back in December when I had to consider selling my home," says Mazeska, who discussed his situation in a series of interviews over the past few weeks. "I was greedy. I had become too confident and I let my ego get the better of me.

Mazeska's riches-to-almost-rags story is an extreme example of the kind of pain felt by millions of investors since last year's market downturn. In hindsight, his mistakes are painfully obvious—Mazeska bought too many stocks on margin, invested too heavily in technology stocks, and waited too long to pay capital-gains taxes on his earlier profits. Maybe worst of all, he believed far too much in his stock-picking prowess.

But there is more to Mazeska's story than just a checklist of investor no-nos. It is a cautionary tale about how online trading can cause investors to lose sight of what buying stocks is all about—investing for the future.

Looking back, however, it is also easy to see how online trading could be so seductive. In 1999 alone, Mazeska posted a $1.46 million portfolio gain. He also had great success managing an investment club—The Desert Storm Investment Club—for himself, his parents, brothers, and a few others. (Before going to college, Mazeska enlisted in the U.S. Marine Corps and saw duty in the Gulf War. He spent most of his tour in a division that built prisoner-of-war camps and cleared land mines.) One of Mazeska's best moves came during the summer of 1999, when he loaded up on 40,000 shares of USWeb/CKS—an Internet consulting firm that is now part of MarchFirst (MRCH). At the time, USWeb's stock was selling around $20. Mazeska sold most of his shares when the stock sprinted to the $40 mark several weeks later—at a profit of $800,000.

But like many investors, Mazeska's golden touch began to disappear last April, when the NASDAQ Composite was hit by the first of several painful sell-offs in technology and Internet stocks. In Mazeska's case, his problem stemmed from a combination of bad timing and bad judgment. Just before the ground began to rumble beneath the NASDAQ, Mazeska made a 175,000-share bet on E*Trade Group (ET), putting almost all his money into the stock. At $26 a share, Mazeska was convinced the online brokerage's stock was greatly undervalued. He says it was intended to be a short-term play, but he felt the stock was due for an extended upward run. Mazeska was so sure of himself that he bought half of those shares on margin, as he had done many times in the past, from his broker, Charles Schwab (SCH).

But within days, the stock skidded to $21. Schwab issued a margin call, and Mazeska was forced to sell $200,000 worth of stock simply to cover the loan. Then he got some more bad news: His accountant told him he owed about $500,000 in taxes on his 1999 capital gains. (Mazeska expected to owe no more than $300,000.) Meanwhile, Mazeska kept hoping his E*Trade stock would rebound. It did not.

"I was down and I wasn't used to that because I had been so successful," says Mazeska. "I was overly confident—I broke all the rules and I should have just sold it all off at once." His accountant, Kenneth Peters, says Mazeska made the mistake of "getting married to a stock" and becoming too enamored of margin buying.

Now, Mazeska realizes that the first thing he should have done in 2000 was pay his 1999 taxes, even if that meant liquidating lots of stock. Instead, he negotiated a monthly installment payment plan with the IRS. But the $30,000-a-month tab proved to be a bit too much, especially when the value of the stocks in Mazeska's account kept sinking. Now he and his lawyers are trying to work out a better payment schedule."

CONSEQUENCES OF TRADING WITHOUT A TRADING PLAN

This is a typical story believe it or not. Now, let us discuss the student who was in my class. We will call him Ben for this story. Ben was married and was young. He decided he wanted to learn more about the currency market because he heard that many people were making a lot of money from the U.S. dollar tanking. Ben wanted to get his share and hopefully retire at a young age from the currency market. On the first day of the class, Ben learned the basics of the Ichimoku indicators. On the second day, we taught him the "ideal" Ichimoku strategy. Before the class, Ben had obtained $10,000 from his wife's account without telling her. He figured he would tell his wife after he made his first $100,000. After the second day of the class, Ben decided to start trading the $10,000. Initially, his first couple of trades were successful and he was easily able to obtain a minimum of 15 pips per trade. Even with the losses he had obtained with the winning trades, those trades had gone up at least 5 pips before they reversed.

After awhile, his confidence rose so high that he decided to increase the contract size and target 3 pips. The next trade, he increased his contract size *drastically*. Unfortunately, it was the wrong trade to do at that particular time. He was instantly down $3,000 within 30 seconds. Apparently, a news announcement was going to be released in the next couple of hours for the currency pair he was trading.

Instead of getting out of the trade, Ben decided to stay in the trade in hopes of recovering the $3,000. He had faith that the currency pair would go up because the higher time frames were all bullish. Not only was Ben down $3,000 but he decided to go to sleep because it was really late and he was tired. Ben had to work early the next morning. Ben went to sleep *without* placing a stop on the order because he had faith it would go up soon.

After a couple of hours of sleep, Ben woke up anxious to see how his trade was working out. It was around 5 A.M. Eastern Standard Time in Atlanta. He looked at his account and the account value was –$2,000 and the account was now "locked" because of the margin call. At 4:30 A.M. EST, a news announcement had been released and the currency he was trading had gapped down. The gap caused his trade to go past the zero instead negative instantly. The brokerage firm could not exit his trade at zero due to the gap. Now, he owed the brokerage firm money. One trade, one night, one loss took him out of trading permanently. He now had to work double just to earn that money back because it was his wife's money.

The question you should ask yourself before reading this chapter is will this be you? Will you have *patience*, *discipline*, and *consistency* to control greed and your emotions? I hope so because trading small time frames moves much faster than trading higher time frames such as the daily charts. If you allow any emotion, that couple of seconds of hesitation can cost a lot of money.

TRADING PLAN

The goal for day trading should be to make a realistic monthly dollar target consistently. The target should be something that puts *no pressure* on your trading. It allows you to have fun while trading. Therefore, a beginner saying they want to make $4,000/month is crazy. The goal for a beginner should be $500/month. After making that amount for six months consistently then you can raise it to $1,000/month, and so forth. Just like a business, expect gradual profit increases not drastic. You will *never* be able to replace a "job" salary for at least two years minimum. Two years is reachable if you work hard at it and maintain discipline.

Let us now get to why you are reading this chapter—how to use Ichimoku Kinko Hyo for day trading. First, we need to create a trading plan around day trading. We will reuse the same trading plan we created earlier with some modifications. Here are the modifications we need to make:

- Our monthly profit target is $250. If we can consistently achieve this profit for six months then we will increase our profit target by $250.
- Only two losses per day are allowed.
- No more than five trades per day can be taken.
- Maximum loss per trade is 25 pips (including the spread).
- Initial capital is going to be $250.
- Contract size allocation for monthly target goals:
  - 1 mini-contract for $250/monthly target.
  - 2 mini-contracts for $500/monthly target.
  - 5 mini-contracts for $1,000/monthly target.
  - 10 mini-contracts for $1,500/monthly target
- Instrument to trade is EURUSD. We choose the EURUSD instrument because the spread that most brokerage firms offer is 2 pips. We need the spread to be low because we are day trading. In day trading, we

cannot expect to get huge price movements. A spread of 10 pips can wipe out our day trading profits especially if we are targeting 15 pips per trade. For higher time frames such as daily, we can allow the spread to be high because our trade goals will be around 200 pips-plus per trade because it is long-term trading.

- Threshold/Stop values
  - Use Kijun Sen with buffer as stop unless the risk is greater than 25 pips. If so, use Tenkan Sen with buffer.
  - Once 12 pips profit has been reached change stop to break even.
  - Once 20 pips has been reached use Tenkan Sen as stop.
  - If bar gaps, exit the trade with minimum 20-pip profit.
- Time frame: 5 minutes.
- Entry stop buffer is 10 pips. After-trade buffer is 5 pips.
- Ichimoku Strategy (Sequence)
  - Kijun Sen cross.
  - Wait for a pullback to Kijun Sen or close to the Kijun Sen.
  - Set up entry trade at exactly at Tenkan Sen.

BACKTESTING

Figure 8.1 shows the first trade on November 17, 2009, for the EURUSD on the 5-minute chart. Table 8.1 shows the trade statistics for this trade. We assume the trading day is from 7 A.M. to 4 P.M. Eastern Standard Time.

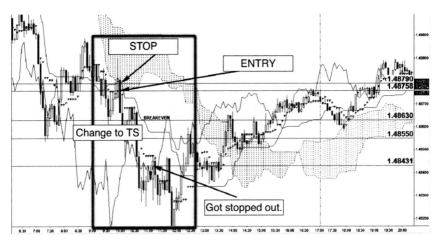

FIGURE 8.1 TradeStation 5 Minute Ichimoku Chart of EURUSD Nov 17, 2009, Trade #1

TABLE 8.1 Trade #1 Statistics

Entry Date	11/17/09
Entry Time	10:00
Entry Price	1.4875
Entry Stop	1.4878 + 0.0010 = 1.4888
Exit Date	11/17/09
Exit Time	11:10
Exit Price	1.4843
Profit	32 pips − spread (0.0002) = 30 pips
Risk	23 pips

The trade was a nice profitable trade. The pullback was to the Kijun Sen and also the bottom of the Kumo Cloud. The bottom of the Kumo Cloud and the Kijun Sen came out to be the same resistance value. Two Ichimoku indicators with two different formulas offer the same resistance value. That is powerful and turns it into a *major* resistance value. The results of the trade are shown in Table 8.1.

In Figure 8.2, you see the second day trade that was taken. Table 8.2 shows the trade statistics. The trade was successful with around 18 pips profit. Notice, you entered the trade before the Kumo Cloud and took profits due to a gap in the 5-minute bar. If you did not exit the trade due to the gap, you would have made around 4 pips. If your trading plan used the Kijun Sen minus a buffer, you would have exited the trade at 1.4864. This is the same price you exited the trade due to the gap.

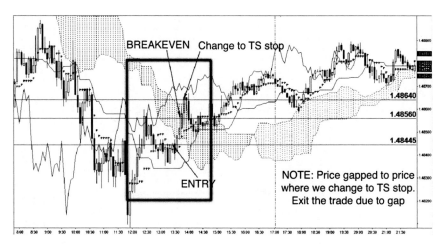

FIGURE 8.2 TradeStation 5 Minute Ichimoku Chart of EURUSD Nov 17, 2009, Trade #2

TABLE 8.2   Trade #2 Statistics

Entry Date	11/17/09
Entry Time	13:25
Entry Price	1.4844
Entry Stop	1.4834 − 0.0010 = 1.4824
Exit Date	11/17/09
Exit Time	13:50
Exit Price	1.4864
Profit	20 pips − spread (0.0002) = 18 pips
Risk	20 pips

The day we selected for backtesting gave us two successful trades. In order to learn, we have to learn from losses. Therefore, we are going to move backward in time to find more days in order to find some losses and examine them. The next date we choose is November 16, 2009, for the 5-minute charts for EURUSD.

Figure 8.3 shows the first day trade for November 16, 2009. This trade was a loss as shown in Table 8.3. Price gapped down drastically crossing over the Kijun Sen. It caused the Tenkan Sen to go down drastically to now become bearish sign. Therefore, we set up for a bearish trade as per our trading plan. The bar after that went higher so it crossed back over the Kijun Sen. It did not go so high that it reached our stop. However, the Tenkan Sen crossed above the Kijun Sen. Therefore, we exited the trade for a loss since that is a bullish sign. If any of the Ichimoku signs change

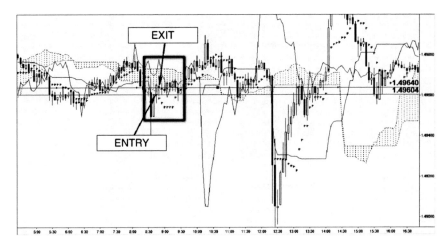

FIGURE 8.3   TradeStation 5 minute Ichimoku Chart of EURUSD Nov 16, 2009, Trade #3

TABLE 8.3	Trade #3 High-Level Statistics
Entry Date	11/16/09
Entry Time	
Entry Price	1.4960
Entry Stop	
Exit Date	
Exit Time	
Exit Price	
Profit	4 pips
Risk	

direction then the trade must be exited right away. This was an ugly trade. The problem from the start was the Tenkan Sen and Kijun Sen relationship. Based on this trade, we definitely know that we may need to change our trading plan to avoid this type of ugly scenario.

The second trade for November 16, 2009, is shown in Figure 8.4. Table 8.4 shows the trade statistics for Trade #4. This trade occurred almost right after the losing trade. The reason is that price was bouncing back and forth on the Kijun Sen during this time period. Remember, our trading plan states that we cannot trade anymore for the rest of the day if we have two losing trades. Therefore, if this trade lost, we would have been done for that day. We added this in our trading plan because there are some days where day trading is just not going to work. On those days, we want to just not trade at all. It is hard for us to recognize those days so we have to trade at least two trades to determine if that day is a nontradable day.

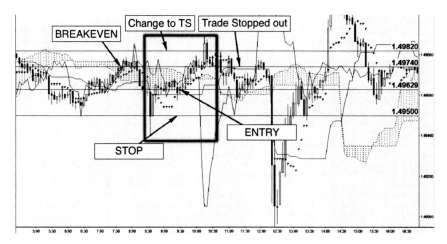

FIGURE 8.4 TradeStation 5 Minute Ichimoku Chart of EURUSD Nov 16, 2009, Trade #4

TABLE 8.4   Trade #4 Statistics

Entry Date	11/16/09
Entry Time	09:30
Entry Price	1.4962
Entry Stop	1.4860 − 0.0010 = 1.4850
Exit Date	11/16/09
Exit Time	10:25
Exit Price	1.4974
Profit	12 pips − spread (0.0002) = 10 pips
Risk	12 pips

Figure 8.5 shows trade #5 for November 16, 2009. The first trade was a loss. The second trade was profitable. Now we are analyzing the third trade for November 16, 2009 which is our fifth trade in total. This trade was very profitable. It was due to a huge gap downward movement. It must have been some type of announcement but either way, we will take it. Table 8.5 shows the trade statistics.

Figure 8.6 shows the fourth potential trade for November 16, 2009. Table 8.6 shows the statistics. We are allowed a maximum of five trades per day. If we can get to five trades per day then it will be a successful day especially if we get three or more winners for that day. For this potential trade, we did not enter it since the pullback was not much at all. We need the pullback to go below the Tenkan Sen in order for us to view it as a pullback.

Figure 8.7 shows the last trade for November 16, 2009. The trade was a loss. Calculate all the values yourself and see if you get a loss.

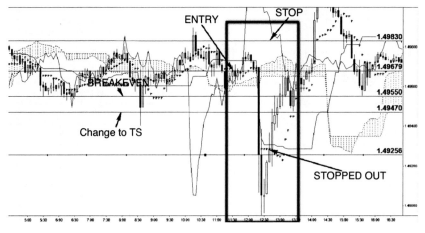

FIGURE 8.5 TradeStation 5 Minute Ichimoku Chart of EURUSD Nov 16, 2009, Trade #5

TABLE 8.5 Trade #5 Statistics

Entry Date	11/16/09
Entry Time	11:35
Entry Price	1.4967
Entry Stop	1.4873 − 0.0010 = 1.4883
Exit Date	11/16/09
Exit Time	12:40
Exit Price	1.4925
Profit	42 pips − spread (0.0002) = 40 pips
Risk	16 pips

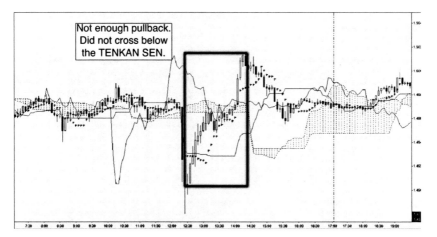

FIGURE 8.6 TradeStation 5 Minute Ichimoku Chart of EURUSD Nov 16, 2009, Potential #6

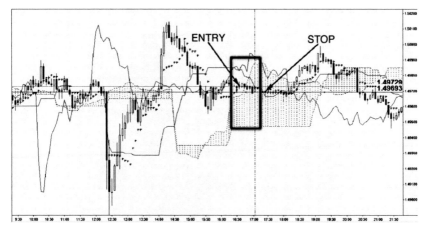

FIGURE 8.7 TradeStation 5 Minute Ichimoku Chart of EURUSD Nov 16, 2009, Actual #6

TABLE 8.6 Trade #6 Statistics

Entry Date	11/16/09
Entry Time	17:05
Entry Price	1.4972
Entry Stop	1.4972 + 0.0010 = 1.4982
Exit Date	11/16/09
Exit Time	18:15
Exit Price	1.4969
Profit	3 pips − spread (0.0002) = 1 pips
Risk	10 pips

CONCLUSION

We are now finished with the day trading backtest. You should have a good idea on how to use Ichimoku Kinko Hyo for day trading. Of course, this is only *one* trading plan around *one* strategy. There are many others. Follow the techniques you have learned to create various trading plans with various day trading strategies. Do not trade a live account until you have a successful backtest.

## CHAPTER 9

Conclusion

We are now at the end of the Ichimoku journey. We have illustrated how to become a successful trader step by step. The process begins just like someone is starting a brand new business, that is, with a business plan. The business plan outlines the business "modules" and how all the modules would be used together to generate revenue and keep expenses to a defined cost. For trading, it is exactly the same way. We create a trading plan instead of a business plan. The trading plan shows step by step how we will trade. It shows the fundamental system, the technical system, money management, assumptions, and so forth, which will be used for trading. This plan will be evaluated at certain times to see that the objectives of the plan have been met. If not, adjustments will be made to get to the end goal. The lessons we have learned in this book are the basic foundations for becoming a good trader. It is up to us to follow the lessons, do the research, do the backtesting, and to *think*.

Our job is complete. I hope the book has been a valuable asset for you. Please provide feedback through our web site www.eiicapital.com. Following is list of web sites that are support tools for you. Please use them. They are there for you to help the journey be a successful one.

Main web site: www.eiicapital.com
Discussion forum: www.kumotrader.com
Blog: www.blog.kumotrader.com
Ichimoku Wiki: www.ichimoku.org

Ichimoku Analysis Sheet

	Ichimoku Trading Questionnaire	
	Date:	
	Instrument:	
	Notes:	
Relationship		**Result**
Price vs. Kumo Cloud		
Bullish or Bearish?	Bullish -> Price above Kumo Cloud	
	Bearish -> Price below Kumo Cloud	
	Consolidation -> Price within Kumo Cloud	
Kumo Shadows	Strong Bullish -> No Shadows	
(Kumo Clouds behind price)	Strong Bearish -> No Shadows	
	Weak Bullish -> Shadow	
	Weak Bearish -> Shadow	

Relationship		Result
Tenkan Sen/Kijun Sen		
Bullish or Bearish?	Bullish -> Tenkan Sen > Kijun Sen	
	Bearish -> Kijun Sen > Tenkan Sen	
	Neutral -> Kijun Sen = Tenkan Sen	
Distance of Price vs. Kijun Sen?	Close -> < (strong)	
	Far -> > (weak)	
Are they in the Kumo Cloud?	Consolidation -> Kijun Sen in Kumo Cloud (weak)	
	Consolidation -> Tenkan Sen in Kumo Cloud (weak)	
	No Consolidation (strong)	
Distance of Price vs. Tenkan Sen?	Close -> (strong)	
	Far -> > (weak)	
Is Kijun Sen flat?	Consolidation -> Flat (weak)	
	Pointing in direction of trend (strong)	
Chikou Span		
Bullish or Bearish?	Bullish -> Chikou above Price (past)	
	Bearish -> Chikou below Price (past)	
Is it in Kumo Cloud?	Consolidation -> Within Kumo Cloud (weak)	
	No consolidation (strong)	
Future Movement (if consolidates, will it run into price)	Will run into price -> Weak Will not run into price -> Strong	
Kumo Future		
Bullish or Bearish?	Bullish -> Senkou A > Senkou B	
	Bearish -> Senkou B > Senkou A	

Relationship			Result
Bullish	**FSA**	**FSB**	
(↑→ pointing up)	↑	—	strong
— → flat	↓	—	weak
↓→ pointing down	↑	↑	strong
FSA → Future Senkou A	—	—	
FSA → Future Senkou B	↓	↑	weak
Bearish	**FSA**	**FSB**	
	↓	—	strong
	↑	—	weak
	↓	↓	strong
	—	—	
	↑	↓	weak
Ichimoku Indicators			
Tenkan Sen (red)	Red -> (Highest High + Lowest Low)/2 for 9 Periods		
Kijun Sen (green)	Green -> (Highest High + Lowest Low)/2 for 26 Periods		
Chikou Span (purple)	Purple -> Current Price projected back 26 periods		
Kumo Cloud			
Senkou Span A	White outline -> (Tenkan Sen + Kijun Sen)/2 projected forward 26 periods		
Senkou Span B	Purple outline -> (Highest High + Lowest Low)/2 for 52 periods projected forward 26 periods		
FOREX			
Buy Entry/Stop	Spread + Buffer		
Sell Entry/Stop	Buffer		

	Website: www.eiicapital.com	
	Blog: www.blog.kumotrader.com	
	DISCUSSION BOARD: www.kumotrader.com	
	WIKI: www.ichimoku.org	

Bibliography

Ichimoku Charts: An Introduction to Ichimoku Kinko Clouds, Nicole Elliott, Harriman Trading, 2007.

Ichimoku Kinko Studies, Hidenobu Sasaki, Toshi Raider Publishing, 1996.

Technical Analysis Explained, 4th ed., Martin Pring, McGraw-Hill, 2002.

Trade Your Way to Financial Freedom, Van K. Tharp, McGraw-Hill, 2007.

Market Forecasting Course, W.D. Gann.

The Missing Peace in Your Life!, Robert M. Williams, M.A., Myrddin Publications, 2004.

www.usatoday.com/educate/college/business/casestudies/20030128-accountingfraud1.pdf.

www.smartmoney.com/investing/stocks/downfall-of-a-day-trader-9916/.

www.1920-30.com/science/television.html.

www.computerhope.com/history/198090.htm.

www.candlecharts.com/.

Charts

All charts were taken from TradeStation. www.tradestation.com

Useful References

Ichimoku Wiki: www.ichimoku.org

Ichimoku Discussion Forum: www.kumotrader.com

Market Technicians Association: www.mta.org

Ichimoku Blog: www.blog.kumotrader.com

E.I.I. Capital: www.eiicapital.com

About the Author

M anesh Patel is a highly respected trader and educator. He graduated with an MS in Electrical Engineering with a minor in Economics. He has worked 16 years in the field of telecommunications and has traveled throughout the world filling roles as sales engineer, development manager, business development, and test engineer.

While working in the field of telecommunications, Manesh's passion has always been trading. He has been trading since 1996. In 2007, Manesh left telecommunication and started to trade full time.

Today, Manesh is a commodity trader advisor and president of E.I.I. Capital Group. He is an Ichimoku trader, educator, and advisor who trades stocks, currencies, futures, options, and so forth, for various global markets. His mission in life is to help everyone become a successful trader.

Index

CPSIA information can be obtained at www.ICGtesting.com
Printed in the USA
BVOW03*1200150813

328469BV00006B/32/P